Upstream
A
Mohawk Valley
Journal

~~~~~~~~~~~~~~~~

A Cultural &
Counter-Cultural
Review

Daniel T. Weaver, Editor

Upstream Publishing
Amsterdam, NY

Dedicated to Edie

who made

this journal possible!

~~~~~~~~~~~~~~~~~~

Additional copies of this journal can be ordered at www.thebookhound.net or by sending a check for $10, made out to Daniel Weaver/The Book Hound, to *Upstream* c/o The Book Hound 16 East Main Street Amsterdam, NY 12010.

ISBN-13: 978-1448605194
ISBN-10: 1448605199

~~~~~~~~~~~~~~~~~~

~~~~~~~~~~~~~~~~~~

Table of Contents

~~~~~~~~~~~~~~~~

Submitting Material To *Upstream*

Upstream is looking for essays, opinion pieces, book reviews, movie reviews and articles on a wide range of subjects for upcoming issues. For more information on how to submit material, check out our blog at www.upstreamjournal@wordpress.com.

~~~~~~~~~~~~~~~~

The Historic Amsterdam League

Upstream is a proud sponsor of The Historic Amsterdam League (HAL). HAL was established in July of 2010 in conjunction with the celebration of the 125th anniversary of the 1885 chartering of the City of Amsterdam, N.Y. HAL is a nonprofit and nonpartisan citizen based organization dedicated to the preservation, promotion, and protection of the physical, cultural, and natural heritage of the City of Amsterdam N. Y. http://www.historicamsterdam.org/

~~~~~~~~~~~~~~~~

From the Editor

In his essay, "A Pluralistic Mystic," philosopher and psychologist, William James, writes of arriving in Amsterdam, New York to visit Paul Benjamin Blood who, long before Timothy Leary was born, was experimenting with drugs, specifically nitrous oxide, and researching their affect on mystical experiences. Of his visit to Amsterdam, James states, "Mr. Blood inhabits a city otherwise, I imagine, quite unvisited by the Muses, the town called Amsterdam, situated on the New York Central Railroad."

No doubt James would have said the same thing if he had stepped off the train in Schenectady, Little Falls or Ilion. But as the first issue of *Upstream* proves, the muses have visited not only Amsterdam but also the entire Mohawk Valley on numerous occasions in the past and the present. One catches a whiff of their perfume in the novels of Walter Edmonds, Harold Frederic, Richard Russo and Joseph Vogel and in the articles, essays and poems that appear in this volume.

Why the title *Upstream*? First, Codman Hislop used the word upstream as a heading in his book, *The Mohawk* (part of the Rivers of America series). Hislop and many other writers have pointed out the Mohawk Valley's importance as the only natural gateway through the mountain barrier that kept Euro-Americans from entering the American heartland. In order to go through the narrow door to the west, one had to travel upstream.

The Mohawk River was the water road to empire. Thousands of Americans and immigrants poured through its valley to seek their fortunes in the west. Without the Mohawk River, the United States might have remained a one-ocean nation, and what we now know as the United States might have been two or three countries.

What was good for the white man, however, was disaster for the various Indian nations scattered across the continent. Today there are only a few Mohawks in the valley, most of them at Kanatsiohareke, the former Montgomery County farm in Yosts. It's not surprising then that many Native Americans look upon what our ancestors did as nothing short of genocide and their lust for land as not much different than the Nazi desire for lebensraum.

Traveling upstream conjures up images of hardship. For both Native Americans and Whites, the Mohawk Valley has not always been an easy place to live. It is not surprising that there are three books about the Mohawk Valley all with almost identical titles referring to the bloody or bloodied Mohawk.

Through bloody conflicts, the Mohawks drove the Algonquins out of the valley, and then the Europeans drove out the Mohawks. The British and French also bloodied each other for control of the valley. Finally, the Americans and the British did the same during the American Revolution, devastating the valley in the process.

Following the Revolution, there was never another military battle in the valley. As the valley industrialized, however, there were battles between capital and labor, which Utica native Harold Frederic wrote about in *The Lawton Girl* and Joseph Vogel wrote about in *Man's Courage*. (More about these two men in the next issue of *Upstream*.) Life was never easy here for the working class.

From an economic viewpoint, life in the valley peaked in the two decades after World War 2. Then the factories began to move out. Since the 1960s, the populations of Amsterdam, Schenectady, Utica and many other valley towns have declined. Once again in the 2010s, we find ourselves jumping high economic hurdles in order to survive.

To go upstream is to go against the current or, to use another metaphor, against the grain. In that respect, the title *Upstream* reflects the counter-cultural aspect of this journal. While many newspapers and magazines are floating downstream belly up, we are swimming upstream in order to spawn a new generation of readers.

The very act of writing poetry or substantive essays—stuff that defies tweeting and texting—is becoming more and more a counter-cultural activity, regardless of content. Publishing a journal that is primary textual, without color, without advertisements, and with few images is counter-cultural too.

The decision to publish this journal on paper rather than in a digital format is also counter-cultural, in spite of the false notion that if we published it digitally we would be "going green." In a few years, the first generation of Kindles and Nooks will enter the landfills to join their forerunners, electronic hand held Bibles and dictionaries that came and went in the 1980s.

Without batteries and electronic parts, this journal cannot break down. Nor will some corporation pressure those who read it to upgrade to a newer model, with lots of extras they either don't need or cannot figure out how to use. And if you tire of *Upstream*, you can recycle it by passing it on to another reader.

Finally, *Upstream* goes against the grain by not following the pattern of the typical regional journal, which only includes articles about that region. As a rule, at least half of *Upstream's* articles will be regional, but we also want to give Mohawk Valley residents the opportunity to express themselves about state, national and international issues. Don't expect *Upstream* to be a re-run of the defunct *Mohawk Valley USA* or *Mohawk Valley Heritage* magazines. We also differ from *Mohawk Valley History*, which is an excellent scholarly journal, that unfortunately ignores the valley east of Herkimer.

Throughout much of its history, the Mohawk Valley has been a polyglot and polyphonic region. It makes sense then that we provide a forum for all points of view. By allowing as many voices to be heard as possible, our hope is that *Upstream* will be a dialogue rather than a monologue, a chorus rather than a solo. This too is counter-cultural. By doing this, we run the risk of alienating dittoheads who only want to read that which confirms what they already believe. The upside of *Upstream*, however, is our readers will be challenged and our writers won't feel they have wasted their time preaching to the choir.

~~~~~~~~~~~~~~~~~~~

Definition of Upstream

"toward or in the higher part of a stream; against the current; in a manner which is contrary to the norm

in the higher part of a stream, closer to the source of the stream"

http://dictionary.babylon.com/upstream/

~~~~~~~~~~~~~~~~~~~

"Slow Train Coming": Oil Depletion and Delusional Thinking

James Howard Kunstler

Everywhere I go these days, talking about the global energy predicament on the college lecture circuit or at environmental conferences, I hear an increasingly shrill cry for "solutions." This is just another symptom of the delusional thinking that now grips the nation, especially among the educated and well-intentioned.

I say this because I detect in this strident plea the desperate wish to keep our "Happy Motoring" utopia running by means other than oil and its byproducts. But the truth is that no combination of solar, wind and nuclear power, ethanol, biodiesel, tar sands and used French-fry oil will allow us to power Wal-Mart, Disney World and the interstate highway system — or even a fraction of these things — in the future. We have to make other arrangements.

Wind farm in Fairfield north of Herkimer

The public, and especially the mainstream media, misunderstands the "peak oil" story. It's not about running out of oil. It's about the instabilities that will shake the complex systems of daily life as soon as the global demand for oil exceeds the global supply. These systems can be listed concisely:

-- The way we produce food

-- The way we conduct commerce and trade

-- The way we travel

-- The way we occupy the land

-- The way we acquire and spend capital

And there are others: governance, health care, education and more.

As the world passes the all-time oil production high and watches as the price of a barrel of oil busts another record, as it did last week, these systems will run into trouble. Instability in one sector will bleed into another. Shocks to the oil markets will hurt trucking, which will slow commerce and food distribution, manufacturing and the tourist industry in a chain of cascading effects.

Problems in finance will squeeze any enterprise that requires capital, including oil exploration and production, as well as government spending. These systems are all interrelated. They all face a crisis. What's more, the stress induced by the failure of these systems will only increase the wishful thinking across our nation.

And that's the worst part of our quandary: the American public's narrow focus on keeping all our cars running at any cost. Even the environmental community is hung up on this. The Rocky Mountain Institute has been pushing for the development of a "Hypercar" for years — inadvertently promoting the idea that we really don't need to change.

Years ago, U.S. negotiators at a U.N. environmental conference told their interlocutors that the American lifestyle is "not up for negotiation." This stance is, unfortunately, related to two pernicious beliefs that have become common in the United States in recent decades. The first is the idea that when you wish upon a star, your dreams come true. (Oprah Winfrey advanced this notion last year with her promotion of a pop book called "The Secret," which said, in effect, that if you wish hard enough for something, it will come to you.)

One of the basic differences between a child and an adult is the ability to know the difference between wishing for things and actually making them happen through earnest effort.

The companion belief to "wishing upon a star" is the idea that one can get something for nothing. This derives from America's new favorite religion: not evangelical Christianity but the worship of unearned riches. (The holy shrine to this tragic belief is Las Vegas.) When you combine these two beliefs, the result is the notion that when you wish upon a star, you'll get something for nothing. This is what underlies our current fantasy, as well as our inability to respond intelligently to the energy crisis.

These beliefs also explain why the presidential campaign is devoid of meaningful discussion about our energy predicament and its implications. The idea that we can become "energy independent" and maintain our current lifestyle is absurd. So is the gas-tax holiday. (Which politician wants to tell voters on Labor Day that the holiday is over?) The pie-in-the-sky plan to turn grain into fuel came to grief, too, when we saw its disruptive effect on global grain prices and the food shortages around the world, even in the United States. In recent weeks, the rice and cooking-oil shelves in my upstate New York supermarket have been stripped clean.

So what are intelligent responses to our predicament? First, we'll have to dramatically reorganize the everyday activities of American life. We'll have to grow our food closer to home, in a manner that will require more human attention. In fact, agriculture needs to return to the center of economic life. We'll have to restore local economic networks — the very networks that the big-box stores systematically destroyed — made of fine-grained layers of wholesalers, middlemen and retailers.

We'll also have to occupy the landscape differently, in traditional towns, villages and small cities. Our giant metroplexes are not going to make it, and the successful places will be ones that encourage local farming.

Fixing the U.S. passenger railroad system is probably the one project we could undertake right away that would have the greatest impact on the country's oil consumption. The fact that we're not talking about it — especially in the presidential campaign — shows how confused we are.

The airline industry is disintegrating under the enormous pressure of fuel costs. Airlines cannot fire any more employees and have already offloaded their pension obligations and outsourced their repairs. At least five small airlines have filed for bankruptcy protection in the past two months. If we don't get the passenger trains running again, Americans will be going nowhere five years from now.

We don't have time to be crybabies about this. The talk on the presidential campaign trail about "hope" has its purpose. We cannot afford to remain befuddled and demoralized. But we must understand that hope is not something applied externally. Real hope resides within us. We generate it — by proving that we are competent, earnest individuals who can discern between wishing and doing, who don't figure on getting something for nothing and who can be honest about the way the universe really works.

Note: This article was first published in 2008. It is reprinted here with the permission of Mr. Kunstler.

James Howard Kunstler is the author of such important non-fiction works as *The Geography of Nowhere*, *Home From Nowhere*, and *The Long Emergency: Surviving the Converging Catastrophes of the 21st Century* as well as many novels. His most recent book, *The Witch of Hebron*, is a sequel to his novel, *The World Made by Hand*. He lives in Saratoga County. His website is http://www.kunstler.com/index.php.

June 27, 1978: Tragedy in Little Falls

Over the years, Little Falls has been the scene of numerous train accidents, including the famous April 19, 1940 Gulf Curve one. On June 27, 1978 tragedy struck again when two adopted Native American boys from Little Falls were found dead on the railroad tracks in nearby Manheim. For years no one knew why they left home without permission, until Chris Billing, their white adoptive brother, researched and made a documentary about them.

The following three articles are about the tragic event in 1978 and the film Chris Billing wrote, directed and produced, *Lost Sparrow*. First, Joseph Bruchac reviews *Lost Sparrow* from a Native American point of view. Then Chris Billing writes about what it was like to return to Little Falls to film and premiere *Lost Sparrow*. Finally, Daniel Weaver writes about sexual abuse and the concept of redemption in *Lost Sparrow*.

While it is helpful, it is not necessary, to have seen the film to enjoy and learn from these essays.

Lost Birds

An essay review of the film *Lost Sparrow*, Written, Produced and Directed by Chris Billing, featuring original music by R. Carlos Nakai. www.lostsparrowmovie.com 2009, Small Handful Productions

Joseph Bruchac, Ph.D

Lost Sparrow, Chris Billing's documentary film that examines a tragic event in his own family's past in Little Falls, New York, can be seen as not one film, but two films in one. The first film is an intensely personal one. It deals with an important part of the filmmaker's own childhood and in doing so lays bare a family secret of the sort that is all too common. Gradually, as the filmmaker tries to find the reason for the tragic deaths of two of his adopted brothers, a secret comes out. His father, a model citizen, a staunch member of their upstate New York Baptist church, was molesting one of his adopted sisters—and the discovery of that molestation was a direct factor in those deaths.

I've seldom seen a movie that deals so directly with this issue. Both his father and mother appear on camera, talking about what happened. His decent mother's classic denial of the fact that her husband has not only been unfaithful to her with other women, but has been molesting one of their ten children—half of whom are adopted— is painful to watch. But so, too, is his father, whose denial and self-justification gradually gives way to an awareness of the enormity of what he has done to their entire family—and a desire to try to make amends, to confess his guilt to and ask forgiveness from the estranged daughter whose life descended into alcoholism and self-hatred after those decades-ago events. It's an important story, one that the filmmaker has shown both great courage and considerable artistry in presenting.

But there is another story here, too. It's one that deals not just with the issues of child abuse and its effects on a family, but with an entire people and a history of another sort of abuse, a societal paternalistic abuse of power fed by assumptions of superiority that goes back centuries. For those two boys who died, the girl who was abused, and her sister Janelle Stands Over Bull—who helped the filmmaker tell this story and whose own story rises to a moment of moving grace at the end—are all members of the Crow Nation of Montana, American Indian children adopted by a well-off white family.

"Lost Sparrows" is a contemporary Native term for Indian children taken away from their people by adoption. And Billings' film does deal to some degree with this phenomenon, which was extremely common during the 1950s and 60s in the United States. But more needs to be said about the issue of the adoption of American Indians by non-native families in states far distant from their ancestral homelands, so much more that I wish there were a viewer's guide to go along with this film for those audiences who do not know about this part of American Indian history.

From 1958 through 1967 there was a program called the Indian Adoption Project. It was administered by the Child Welfare League of America and funded by federal money through the Bureau of Indian Affairs. Its purpose was to place Native children from sixteen western states with "well-matched" white families in several states in the East and Midwest. Hundreds of Indian children were adopted out. Nearly all of them came from communities where extended Native families (that would gladly have taken in those children) were the rule. Many of them, like Billings' brothers Bobby and Tyler and his sisters Lana (who was the abuse victim) and Janelle still had living parents.

The Indian Adoption Project had powerful advocates in the bureaucratic and social science communities. It was seen as a step forward, a sign of the decrease of American racial prejudice that white families would willingly adopt Indian children. David Fanshel, a child welfare researcher, actually published in 1972 a book called *Far From The Reservation*, that concluded in no uncertain terms that the vast majority of adopted Indian children and their families adjusted well.

However, by the 1970s, American Indian activists were challenging the assumptions of that practice. Like the Indian boarding schools of the late 19th and first half of the 20th century that took children from their homes and placed them under harsh military discipline with the stated aim to "kill the Indian and save the man," the adoption project was just another in a long line of genocidal practices aimed at wiping out Indian culture and identity.

As a result, in 1978 Congress passed the Indian Child Welfare Act, which defined American Indian children as collective resources essential to tribal survival and made such adopting out practices no

A 1972 family photo, taken shortly after the four Crow Indian children, Bobby, Lana, Tyler and Janelle, were adopted.

longer easy. There are now significant barriers to non-native families or anyone without tribal affiliation to adopt Native American children.

To be fair, the life that Chris Billings' adopted siblings left behind was a difficult one. His interviews with their biological father —who had been a promising athlete before injuries ended his sports career—show that he was far from fit to care for, or perhaps even care about, those four children, fathered during his teenage years. They needed rescuing from neglect. And that all of them were adopted out together was a measure of the agencies that arranged their adoption caring about their feelings. But not their culture.

There were uncles and aunts who mourned the loss of those children and whose eloquent voices are also part of the documentary. And when the two older brothers of Lana, Bobby aged 13 and Tyler aged 11, learned about the fact that their little sister was being sexually molested, they stated that they hated their adopted father. They told Lana that they would help her. And then they ran away from home.

Perhaps they were hoping to get to Montana to find relatives and ask them for the help they could not get from an adopted mother deep in denial and an adopted father they now feared. But they did not go far. Both were struck and killed by a train, perhaps a train they had planned to hop and ride west. And it is was not until the making of this film that Chris Billings' father either accepted or even realized that his actions were the catalyst that led to their deaths.

The distance between the world from which those four children were taken and the "privileged" life of a well-meaning but tragically flawed white family could not be more dramatic. And the fact that the white part of the Billings family during the filmmaker's youth did not seem to have a clue, not one, about so many things--the sexual abuse, the results of their actions or inactions, the culture that the native children had left behind, the whole history of unequal relations between Indians and majority culture makes this film even more poignant--and important to see. Everything that this film portrays--on all levels--is still going on.

As Chris Billings oversees the exhumation of his dead brothers, as he drives a rented van across American to return them to the Crow lands of the family and nation that have not forgotten them or stopped longing for their return, we may recognize that this is not the past that we are seeing. This is a glimpse into the divided hearts of the peoples of our first nations, of America itself.

Joseph Bruchac is a poet, storyteller, and author of more than sixty books as well as hundreds of magazine articles. He is the recipient of the American Book Award, the PEN Syndicated Fiction Award and the Lifetime Achievement Award from the Native Writers' Circle of The Americas. Mr. Bruchac lives with his family in Greenfield Center, New York. His website is http://www.josephbruchac.com/.

Sometimes You Can Go Home Again

Chris Billing

I felt anxious as I drove along the New York State Thruway in August 2009. The documentary I had just finished, *Lost Sparrow*, was making its Little Falls, NY premiere that evening, and I had no idea what to expect. I didn't know if people would come out to watch a film about the tragic deaths of two Crow Indian brothers on the outskirts of town more than three decades earlier. I suspected that, by now, most Little Falls residents had no memory of the sad events that devastated my family all those years ago.

At the time, though, their deaths dominated local news. The *Little Falls Evening Times* headline on June 27, 1978, shouted "Two Local Boys Killed By Train." Scores of police, firefighters, Boy Scouts, and others had searched frantically the night before, after my adopted brothers Bobby, 13, and Tyler, 11, were reported missing.

Tyler, Bobby, Lana and Janelle, taken shortly before their adoption by the Billing family.

A few days later, hundreds of people — including many of my brothers' classmates — packed the Little Falls Baptist Church for their closed-casket funeral. I was 16 at the time, and I remember feeling flushed and dizzy as I tried to carry my share of the weight as a pallbearer. Their bronze caskets were much heavier that I expected. My mother asked me if I needed help, but I said no.

My family had always been an anomaly in the small, upstate New York town. My mother liked to call us "the von Trapps of Little Falls." We outnumbered the children in *The Sound of Music* by three, and a family of ten wasn't entirely out of the ordinary in a predominantly Catholic community. But my siblings included five Native Americans—one Apache from Arizona and four Crow siblings from Montana—and that was certainly unusual in a mostly Irish and Italian town.

And then, of course, there was the house.

I was 10 and about to enter 5th grade in the summer of 1972, when my family packed up and moved from suburban New Jersey into the Overlook Mansion—a sprawling Victorian castle with 12 bedrooms on a hillside above Little Falls.

The Overlook Mansion Little Falls, NY

The years that followed I remember as mostly idyllic. Little Falls is a quaint, quiet, old-fashioned town on the Erie Canal where everybody know everybody's business, and people see no reason to lock their doors. I learned quickly never to say anything bad about anybody, since it was likely that the person to whom I was complaining was somehow related to the person I was complaining about.

My family adjusted quickly to life in Little Falls. My brothers and sisters and I played on sports teams and worked on our expansive cattle farm. We went "down street" to hang out with friends (I'm still not sure why we called it that), and, as we got older, went drinking on "the roads." (Among my classmates, I remain legendary for my inability to hold my alcohol.) Every winter we skied on Shumaker Mountain. In summer we waterskied at our "camp" in the Adirondacks.

Not long after I left for college in the mid-1980s, though, my parents sold the Overlook property and moved the family back to New Jersey. My mother worried that, as her children grew up and moved away, she would end up rattling around in that huge house alone.

But without family to visit in Little Falls, it became harder to make the long trek up there. Contact with my childhood friends dwindled.

In late March 2007, I returned to Little Falls for the first time in decades to begin researching *Lost Sparrow*. Unsurprisingly, the town seemed smaller and less imposing than the Little Falls of my memories. But in fact very little had changed. The shops along Main Street had new names, but the old layout remained. I was pleased to discover that many friends from childhood had stayed local. Several ran flower shops, restaurants, bars and other businesses around town.

My production crew and I ended up making several trips to Little Falls during the making of *Lost Sparrow*. We filmed at Overlook Mansion and various locations around town, and scanned microfilm at the local library for *Evening Times* articles about my brothers' deaths. We interviewed local police who had investigated the incident, and I was touched that every one of them broke down in recounting that morning.

I frequently bumped into people around town who had known my family, and they invariably asked about my parents and siblings. I began to feel as if I had never left.

Finally, on October 15, 2007, nearly 30 years after their deaths, we disinterred my brothers' remains at the Rural Park Cemetery in Manheim, NY, loaded their coffins into a U-Haul, and started the long journey to the Crow Reservation in Montana to bury them on their ancestral land. That wrapped the Little Falls portion of our film production.

What followed were two years of location shooting in Montana, Florida, New Jersey and North Carolina, countless writes and rewrites of the script, many months of editing in a darkened edit suite, and a grand premiere in Park City, UT.

Finally, I was driving back to Little Falls to show *Lost Sparrow* in the town where the events had occurred. I arrived at the Valley Cinema Theater an hour or so early to check sound and make sure everything was set up properly. When I went back into the theater lobby, I was overwhelmed to discover that the line stretched out the door and across the parking lot. We ended up having three standing-room-only screenings that Thursday night, and added a fourth on Saturday morning.

I was gratified by the strong response to the film. Each screening was followed by a vibrant discussion, including numerous stirring and heart-felt testimonials about my family. We were clearly remembered fondly. Later, one high school buddy wrote me eloquently about the "special bond" that endures between close friends from the past. I couldn't agree more.

Chris Billing has more than two decades of experience in documentary filmmaking and network news coverage. He worked for more than a decade as a China-based journalist, including a five-year stint as Beijing Bureau Chief for NBC News (1996-2001). His first documentary, *Up To The Mountain, Down To The Village*, (2005), returned with three members of China's "lost generation" to the remote and impoverished villages where they were sent as teenagers for a decade of re-education during Chairman Mao's tumultuous Cultural Revolution. For more information about Billing and how to purchase *Lost Sparrow* and *Up To The Mountain*, check out http://chrisbilling.com/.

Sexual Abuse and the Concept of Redemption in *Lost Sparrow*

Daniel Weaver

When my son and I attended the Little Falls premiere of *Lost Sparrow* at the packed Valley Cinema in 2009, we both agreed that it was one of the most powerful documentaries we had ever seen, and we have watched hundreds of them. Following the show, my son purchased a copy of the film on dvd, and I have watched it several times since.

We are not alone in our positive assessment of *Lost Sparrow*. PBS believed it was worthy of showcasing on its Emmy Award winning Independent Lens. *Lost Sparrow* also won the Best Documentary Feature at the 2009 American Indian Film Festival, Best Indigenous Voices award at the 2011 Fargo Film Festival and has been nominated for several other awards.

As powerful and moving as it is, the film raises as many questions as it answers. The obvious one is why were Tyler and Bobby Billing on the railroad tracks on June 27, 1978, the day they were run over by a train. One police officer suggests that the previous night had been cool, and they were warming themselves from the heat radiating from the crushed stone of the rail bed and fell asleep on the tracks. Another officer suggested they were trying to hop a train. In any event, there is no sure and satisfactory answer to the question.

And there are no satisfactory answers to a number of other important questions the film raises.

The most troubling questions that the film raises are about Mr. and Mrs. Billing, the film maker's parents. The film maker, Chris Billing, doesn't always ask the questions that we want answered, but that is not meant to be a criticism of him. Its a rare documentarian who will look at his family under a microscope as Billing did. It was a painful experience, and Billing admitted afterward that he would never have made the film if he had known ahead of time what he was getting into.

Until the making of this film, Stu Billing, the film maker's father, does not appear to realize the havoc he wreaked on his family, or that he is a perfect example of the proverb "Whoever troubles his ousehold, reaps the wind." But if Stu Billing reaps the wind, it be in the next life because it seems that in this life he got away n being an incestuous child molester. Indeed, the most asked and answered question in the Talkback forum of Independent Lens was why wasn't Stu Billing in prison. No satisfactory answer has been given.

If Stu Billing reaped the wind, his family has reaped the whirlwind.

Two children dead.

One child scarred for life by incest.

The other children left with conflicting emotions about their father.

The subtitle of the film, *Innocence Stolen, Redemption Found*, raises the question as to whether or not redemption is found. The film's climactic scene in which Mr. and Mr. Billing and several of their now adult children meet with the victimized adopted daughter to attempt reconciliation is the weakest and most troubling part of the documentary. The burden of the meeting seems to fall on the victim and whether or not she will forgive her adoptive father, rather than on the father and the evil of his actions.

The meeting seems forced. It appears to meet some spiritual need the mother has for closure, and possibly the film maker's personal and professional need to create a happy ending to an otherwise unrelenting unhappy story. While the father does come to realize during the process of making this documentary that he was indirectly responsible for the deaths of Bobby and Tyler and does show some remorse over it, he never seems to fully comprehend all that he has done.

There is a strange disconnect between Stu Billing and his conscience and between Stu Billing and his emotions. He expresses anger that Bobby and Tyler ran away and caused the family trouble, yet he is able to put himself in the shoes of the train engineer who ran over them, expressing more empathy and sorrow for him than anyone else in the story.

Neither he nor his wife ever call Bobby and Tyler their sons. They are always referred to as the boys, the two boys or something similar.

Also, not revealed in the film, but revealed on the Independent Lens' website is that:

> "Bobby and Tyler Billing ran away on a Monday. Their bodies were discovered on the train tracks on Tuesday. They were buried on Wednesday. Their family moved to their summer home on Thursday and barely spoke of the boys again."

Everyone handles death differently differently, and while we must be careful about judging people for their behavior following the death of a loved one, Mr. Billing's behavior following the deaths of his two sons seems to indicate either he was a callous person or that he had guessed that the boys were planning to expose his crimes when they ran away.

The viewer can understand and empathize some with Mrs. Billing when he realizes that she was married to a controlling and emotionally abusive husband whom she eventually separated from and divorced. Nevertheless, some of her words and actions are troubling. At one point in the film, she says she did not know what her husband did to their daughter. On another occasion, she says she looked through the keyhole in the bathroom door and saw him fondling her, opened the door and confronted him.

She says she put safeguards in place so it wouldn't happen again. But then she wakes up one night and finds that her husband is not in bed. She assumes wrongly that he is with one of his girlfriends. Whatever safeguards she may have put in place, they could not have been very effective since the abuse continued into the daughter's teen years.

What Lost Sparrow presents in the form of redemption, at least in the Christian sense of the word, is partial. For redemption to take place, both parents needed to fully own their behavior—the father his abuse and incest, the mother her enabling. Neither parent quite does that.

They must own up to their sins prior to and regardless of whether or not their victim forgives them. To do otherwise is to cheapen grace, forgiveness and redemption. However, the parents' needs seem to take precedence over the needs of their daughter. The forgiveness that the daughter extends to her father near the end of the film seems forced out of her, and she makes conflicting statements about whether or not she forgives him. If not given of her free will, it is not true forgiveness. And the mother does not seem to fully realize that she too needs to be forgiven for what she did, or neglected to do, for her daughter.

Lost Sparrow was released two years ago. Like many a good independent documentary, it struggles to be seen and heard among the glitz and din of action packed, noisy but empty Hollywood films. Unlike most of those films, *Lost Sparrow* is worth watching and re-watching. Just don't approach it with the idea that the film will provide you with catharsis or that it will bring closure to the many tragedies it discloses.

~~~~~~~~~~~

Notable Mohawk Valley Quote

"This is Te-non-an-at-che, "the river flowing through mountains," the Mohawk, along whose banks France failed to win great allies in the fight to dominate America, and England lost her key battle to hold the Thirteen Colonies. This river and its valley are worth knowing."

"This is the river that cut a gate through the rock wall of the Appalachian Plateau, the only entrance into the Western Plains between Georgia and the St. Lawrence Valley. Let your imagination dwell on that one fact for a moment. As tides flow over the land, so, too, did streams of men flow north from the Atlantic seaboard up the forested basin of the Hudson to the Mohawk Valley, and then west into Genesee country, the Great Lakes country, and the seemingly limitless America beyond."

"Struggle and battle on a hundred levels took place to possess this river valley. To possess it meant to possess America."

From *The Mohawk* by Codman Hislop

Begorra! Amsterdam, not NYC, Home to New York's First St. Patrick's Day

Robert von Hasseln

Amsterdam, New York, whose residents have long held it superior to New York City in many regards (such as carpet making and alphabetical order), can now lay claim to yet another accomplishment: that of being the site of the first recorded Saint Patrick's Day secular celebration in what is today New York State.

Buried in fourteen volumes of papers relating to Sir William Johnson, published by the State of New York in the early 20th Century, is a letter from Johnson to the royal governor of New York written on March 18, 1747, reporting:

> *We kept S[t]* [Saint] *Patrick yesterday & this Day Y[r]* [your] *Health & all freinds* [sic] *in Albany W[th]* [with] *so many other Healths* [toasts], *I Can Scarce write…*

Historians generally regard the first Saint Patrick's Day celebration in New York City as being a spontaneous parade of Irish soldiers in British units stationed there in 1762; the first organized observance was a dinner at the Crown and Thistle Inn in 1766. The first ever in America (and probably worldwide) was in Boston, only ten years before the one in Amsterdam. (The first parade in Ireland was in 1931, and pubs were closed by law on Saint Patrick's Day there until the 1970s).

The house in which the 1747 merrymaking occurred is long gone. Johnson's original home, after he moved from the south side of the Mohawk River to the north around 1740, was remodeled circa 1764 to accommodate his daughter and her husband, Daniel Claus. Claus became a notorious Loyalist during the Revolution and local patriots torched his home after he fled into British service. Later, the ruins were obliterated by newer structures and ultimately the New York Central Railroad. Today the Amsterdam train station occupies roughly the same site.

Johnson's observance was not a one-time thing. Also in the collected papers is this from his brother Warren's 1761 journal:

March the 17ᵗʰ. Cold frosty Weather. A great Meeting
at my Brother's House to drink St. Patrick, & most got
vastly drunk.

And from Johnson's account with Gilbert Tice, a local merchant, in 1774:

17ᵗʰ March   To 2 gallons of beer for Yᵉ [the] foot Ball
players 8 [shillings] 0 [pence].

More alcohol, but also one of the earliest references to sport in Colonial America and an indication that the holiday at Johnson's home involved more than drinking. Other references in the collection allude to contests and prizes: hidden money for children to search for, greased pole climbing (often won by Mohawk boys) and a story of a greased pig chase in which an older Mohawk woman outfoxed younger warriors by coating her hands in wet sand.

In this way, Johnson's Saint Patrick's Days were more reflective of modern America practice than many of the Saint Patrick's Days that came in between. A diverse society (Scots, Germans, English, Dutch, and Native Americans) coming together to share an Irish holiday, rather than the earlier Irish-only occasions which emphasized solidarity, civil rights and recognition.

Although the earliest recorded, 1747 was probably not the first time William Johnson celebrated Saint Patrick's Day in the wilderness. That year, he was heavily involved in the prosecution of the third (King George's War) of four wars before the Revolution we call collectively the French and Indian Wars. On the same day he wrote of the Saint Patrick's festivities, he was also receiving the return of a colonist/Native American scouting party from around Saratoga and preparing to dispatch other war parties against the French. It's likely he established the custom in his household in calmer times before the war began in 1744.

But not much earlier: while the young immigrant from County Meath (original family name: McShane [John's Son]) held close the Catholic traditions of his youth (despite converting to Anglicanism to pursue his future in the British Empire), his first years on the frontier were spent consolidating his position. Too Catholic an appearance would have been unwise: Catholic Masses were still illegal in New

York and priests subject to arrest. That Saint Patrick was also the patron saint of the Anglican Church of Ireland probably helped.

Johnson's rise to power was meteoric and his part pivotal to the development of what would become the United States. Later a major general, Superintendant of Indian Affairs, and one of only four "colonials" to be knighted by the British King, he was lord of New York's frontier in all but name. In time, he would use that power to settle hundreds of Catholics on his lands and shelter their priest and ceremonies from other colonial authorities.

Sir William Johnson died on the eve of the American Revolution. Most of his heirs and supporters fled to Canada and the British cause after hostilities began. Despite this, decades later the first federal census (1790), revealed that over a third of New York's Irish lived in Albany and Montgomery Counties; the rest were spread among the Hudson Valley, New York, and Long Island. The great urban Irish populations lay well in the future. So it's not surprising that the first Saint Patrick's Day in New York was on the banks of the Mohawk, not the East River; only that we don't celebrate that fact as we celebrate the day.

Other Johnson family homes that hosted later celebrations still remain and are open to the public: Old Fort Johnson (1749; Village of Fort Johnson; Montgomery County Historical Society), Johnson Hall (1763; Johnstown; Johnson Hall State Historical Site), and Guy Park Manor (1766; Amsterdam; Water Elwood Museum).

Visitors to these sites can be excused if, even without the benefit of drink or heritage, they hear echoes of different peoples, old and new, coming together in the primeval forest that once was Amsterdam, to revel in their shared release from winter's hold and Lenten obligations by celebrating the patron saint of their patron's homeland.

Robert von Hasseln is the City of Amsterdam Historian, founder of the Historic Amsterdam League and co-author with Gerald Snyder of *A Postcard History of Amsterdam*.

~~~~~~~~~~~~~~~~~~

"Looking A Gift Horse:" A Personal Essay

K. Wayne

It was the first snowfall of this winter, and my wife and daughter and I were walking to the car.

"Step in the footprints daddy made earlier so you don't get snow in your shoes." my wife said.

As I watched my daughter, in the twilight of her teen years, stretching her thin legs beyond their normal stride to walk in my footsteps, I felt the hammer under my third rib strike hotter and harder than usual. And I knew that what ever happens in life, I have to do the right thing—sometimes the hard thing—because eventually the sun will come out, and my footsteps will be lost to her forever.

And then a few days later, I was in our computer room and I saw a beautifully bound book with a sewn in bookmark on the cot. I picked it up to see what it was, opened it and found words in my daughter's handwriting which said I was the person she most respected in the world. I slammed the book shut, feeling bad that I had invaded someone's privacy but feeling good about what I had read.

And it happened again on Christmas Day. My wife gave me a letter, instead of a card, because she couldn't find a card that said what she wanted to say. And the letter said in part, "You are the yardstick I would like our children to measure what a man is by."

Who could ask for a nicer Christmas present than that?

The truth is that all three events were precious gifts to a middle-aged man. Middle age can be a scary time for both men and women. Nothing is what it used to be. In a single night, the temperature can drop and black ice glaze your dreams. Already your body and brain are beginning to fail you in subtle ways. Your children are leaving home. You become restless with your job or get laid off and no one wants to hire you. And if you have a job, you worry about how you will make it when you retire. Worst of all, many of the self doubts of adolescence erupt again like a bad case of acne.

Then a stranger enters your life and you look into her eyes and see the stark beauty of swamps and marshlands, the owl meditating in a dead tamarack, the water below unmoving, silent, seemingly empty of life to the careless passerby, but brimming to the more observant.

Maybe you've been married for twenty-five or thirty years. For all those long years you never climbed over fences or rock walls to trespass on your neighbor's pastures or even neighed at your neighbor's wife. Sure, when you were younger, you often looked at the bodies of other women and felt strong longings. But they were no more than the springtime longings of a stallion—blind reflexes—the doctor hitting just below the kneecap with a rubber mallet and the leg springing forward with no will of its own.

So why not wade into the deep waters? Everyone else seems to be doing it. A governor from another state runs off to Argentina, not telling anyone where he is going, and makes an ass of himself. Two of your former governors have turned the television set into a confessional booth.

But you know that kind of thing is not for you. You can't slink around behind your spouse's back, no longer able to look into her eyes. No sordid visit to a motel for you, followed by rumpled sheets in the morning and the weary feeling that what you got was not really what you were looking for.

Besides, the woman is not a tramp. She is a lady. And your wife is a lady. And you know full well you would be the worst kind of bastard if you betrayed either one of them.

So you pull back from the edge of those deep waters—thankful however for those sweet words that removed some of your self doubts —but knowing also that many men and women have drowned themselves in similar waters.

And you realize that what you first saw when you looked into the depths of those eyes—what you thought you fell in love with— was not someone else, but your own image reflected in them. And you realize also that you haven't lost anything by not diving in. True love is still there, in that pure mountain stream that you drank from and swam in for decades, and that knocked you off your feet the first time you waded into it so many, many years ago.

K. Wayne is the pen name of a longtime Mohawk Valley resident.

~~~~~~~~~~~~~~~

Hollywood Beds

Linda Ciulik Wisniewski

We must have been eight or ten years old when the beds arrived.

"We got the girls Hollywood beds," my father told the neighbors and my sister, and I knew from his tone they were special. The white plastic headboards embossed with jewel-like facets were pierced by golden studs. In later years, I would see Doris Day and Rock Hudson romp around beds like these on the big screen at the Rialto Theater downtown. Along with the blond dresser that barely fit inside the room, our furniture spoke of luxury. We had a little money, our own home and Hollywood beds.

Our lives back then were furnished in shiny plastic. White linoleum with red, black and gold flecks covered the floor of our bedroom. In summer, my mother hung thin plastic curtains in a dizzying white and red print over two small windows open to the breeze. A small closet with a dowel across the middle held two rows of little girls' clothes. How few they were: a dress or two for church, dark green school uniforms and white blouses, a couple of pairs of shoes on the floor. Play clothes for after school and weekends. The dresser held our socks and underwear, and everything I wore was handed down to my younger sister.

A few years later, in the early 1960s, a developer built ranch homes on the northern edge of town. My father read with reverence the name on a street sign, "Hollywood Road," each time we drove by. He often spoke of movie stars in casual conversation, though I don't recall ever going to the Rialto with him.

It was Mom who took us to see *Bambi, Fantasia, Snow White,* all the Disney animated features. Once, she took me to see a rather adult movie, *A Star Is Born,* starring James Mason and Judy Garland. I was named, she said, for the actress Linda Darnell.

With Dad, we watched movies on TV. *Peter Pan*, *The Wizard of Oz* and *The Sound of Music*, and in his own odd departure from children's fare, Ernest Borgnine in *Marty*. Fragments of his words come back to me: "Deanna Durbin, what an actress!" "Frank Sinatra, the greatest singer of all time!" "That Bob Hope, what a comedian!"

Kirk Douglas' Birthplace Amsterdam

Like everyone who lived in Amsterdam, New York, we knew the story of Isadore Demsky, our favorite son who became the actor Kirk Douglas. Mom said she often heard his Russian immigrant father calling out "Rags! Rags!" as he drove his horse and wagon down the street.

My father sang Nat King Cole's hit, "Paper Moon," to my mother soon after they met, like most couples in town, at the rug mill. Amsterdam was Rug City then, home to Mohawk Carpets and the Bigelow-Sanford Company, and well into my childhood, the town was prosperous. But one January day in 1955, the local radio interrupted its program with a news bulletin: Bigelow-Sanford was moving to Connecticut. Before the 1960s ended, Mohawk Carpets headed south where labor was cheap. The Rug City no longer made rugs.

In the following decades, the empty factory buildings were partially occupied by manufacturers of plastic swimming pools, men's pants, and in a brief flurry of hope for a prosperous future, the packing and shipping of Cabbage Patch dolls made in China. By the time

Hollywood Road was built, my father worked at the General Electric plant in Schenectady. It was there, in the steam turbine division, he injured his back. His factory days and larger paychecks were no more.

He found a job as a warehouse security guard at night and on weekends, but my parents argued over the small tools and hardware he brought home from the endless rows of bins he guarded. I wonder now what he was thinking. He was fired when the thefts were discovered and hid his shame behind a loud-mouthed bluster that descended into verbal and emotional abuse. Nothing could please him or make him happy. My sister and I cut our food wrong, scraping the knife too loudly on the plate. Mom was "stupid" and "a lousy cook." And somewhere in that time, somebody poked a hole in one of the Hollywood beds.

Surprisingly after the petty theft, a local bank hired Dad as their janitor. One of his duties was to greet the manager every day by his first name, "Good morning, Tom," but if a robbery was in progress, there would be a secret message. He was to say "Good morning, Mr. Butler." My father was very proud of this responsibility, and I heard him rehearse the greeting often, though he never had to use it.

Both his brothers were city aldermen, and they encouraged him to run for office as well, but Mom was against it. She didn't want "people coming to the house at all hours," she said. He wrote eloquent letters to the editor of the newspaper but even this amount of attention annoyed my mother. "He has another letter in the *Recorder*," she muttered. "What will people say?"

Some evenings my father's friend Marshall stood on our front step as they talked local politics through the aluminum screen door. Mom didn't want him in the house. My sister and I didn't know what to make of this as tension between our parents hung over the house with the Hollywood beds, the house where only close relatives were allowed inside.

I don't know why my father didn't run for office or let his friend in despite my mother's protests. Instead, he shouted angry words at us and ate too much, until he was obese and embarrassing to Mom. "He wasn't fat when I married him," she explained.

Long after my sister and I left home, the beds with the plastic headboards remained in our empty room in the little white house. The hole was patched with brown packing tape – plastic, of course.

"Throw that thing out, Mom," I said when I went back to visit. "It's depressing."

"Why?" she responded with a frown. "It's a perfectly good bed."

As time went on, my hometown struggled to restore its faded glory. Ideas came and went. The stores on Main Street where my friends and I bought lipstick and ice cream sodas were replaced by a mall, now all but deserted. A developer wanted to turn an old factory into upscale apartments, but the city council voted to tear it down. A Buddhist group bought an abandoned elementary school, two churches and more than 40 houses but left town after some buildings were vandalized. In the East End, Latinos opened groceries in abandoned storefronts, but older residents blame these newest immigrants for a rise in crime.

Dairy cows and red barns still perch on softly rolling hills just a mile or two from the center of town. The long wide ribbon of the Mohawk River splits the city in two. Up the steep hills to the north, powerful creeks crash noisily over rocks outside the now abandoned rug mill where my parents met. They say the creeks turned red and blue on the days they dyed the yarn.

My friends and I lament the loss of Rapello's Drugs and Holzheimer's Department Store, and imagine we once lived in a town like Bedford Falls in *It's a Wonderful Life*, but history tells a different story. In his 1988 memoir, *The Ragman's Son*, Kirk Douglas wrote that Jews like his father were barred from working in the mills.

It makes me sad to think of it, and of my own father, who tried to buy us some Hollywood glamour when all we longed for was his approval. After the mills closed, the population dropped and the Rialto closed its doors. There are no movie theaters left in Amsterdam today.

On weekday mornings, a line of cars moves across the river, bound for the Thruway and jobs in other towns. Under the bridge, the mighty Mohawk still sparkles in the sun.

Linda Ciulik Wisniewski grew up in Amsterdam but now lives in Bucks County, PA where she writes features for a weekly newspaper and teaches memoir writing workshops. She is the author of *Off Kilter, A Woman's Journey To Peace With Scoliosis, Her Mother & Her Polish Heritage*. Her website is www.lindawis.com.

From Fundamentalism to Feminism:
A Journey - Part One

Ruth Peterson

From earliest childhood through early married life, I was a Christian fundamentalist. There was nothing else to be in my family. On both sides, my relatives were all strong fundamentalists. No black sheep here. The men were not mere mortal men; they were "saints," as in "Your grandfather was a saint." The women, while less revered for their faith, (purity comes naturally to women) quietly raised the children, obeyed their husbands, took care of the sick, entertained missionaries, taught Sunday School, read their Bibles and prayed. The seeds for my future feminism were thus rooted in this patriarchal belief system.

All of life was suffused with the sights, sounds, smells, tastes and texture of fundamentalism. My first olfactory memory is the tangy smell of fine white sand from the seashore in the church's primary room sandbox. Then there was the smell of toast and starched linen at my grandmother's house as we knelt by our chairs after breakfast while my grandfather prayed. There was the Easter morning scent of lilies and hyacinths banking the altar as we gathered for the Sunrise Service and the smell of pine needles and slightly damp bedding at the various summer Bible camps we attended. And later, the smell of yeast rolls and coffee rising as we stood behind our chairs waiting for morning prayer in the college dining room before we could eat.

Also embedded in my brain are the deep resonant masculine tones of countless ministers, missionaries and evangelists who filled the pulpits of my youth—enough rhetoric to last a lifetime. I recall the florid, grandiloquent speech they used for delivering sermons and the hushed reverent tones they employed at the conclusion to issue the "invitation to accept Christ." Both tonal qualities challenged the young to either submit or be damned. I marvel now at my childish fortitude in the face of tortured self-examination during those altar calls. I decided that I had been "saved" by some early, private act of self-determination that I could or would not display for a crowd. But I shuddered in recognition when I read the words of Mrs. Kemper Campbell:

"Oh Kind, Oh Just, Oh Merciful
What then shall be their shame
Who taught a little child
To tremble at Thy name."

Tremble we did, before God and all his male representatives.

For the child that I was, the music of fundamentalism was most seductive. The soul and spirit of a child is a tender thing. My spirit was quieted by hymns like "The Old Rugged Cross," "I Come to the Garden Alone," "Pass Me Not, Oh Gentle Savior" and "Be Still My Soul." At other times, we were aroused to something like militancy as we sang "Onward Christian Soldiers," "A Mighty Fortress Is Our God," "The Battle Hymn of the Republic" or "God of Our Fathers," which opens with trumpet or organ flourishes. Many of the old hymns still come unbidden often at the end of day: "Lead, Kindly Light, Amid the Encircling Gloom" and "Abide With Me, Fast Falls the Eventide." We were always imploring a Higher Being for safety and comfort.

The texture of life in a fundamentalist family included, in addition to all our blood relatives, those kindly sincere adults who shared our beliefs. Paul, the large, gentle German baker who stood at every Thursday night prayer meeting and spoke his "testimony" in broken English. Ivy, the pretty young minister's wife whose every deed was a tribute to her handsome, dynamic husband, and the red-haired spinster, Rhoda, who taught the girl's Sunday School class and whose only words that remain with me today are "Never set your heart on anything. Pray for God's will, not your own, and then you will never be disappointed." I can only imagine the lifetime of disappointment she had endured.

Our devout maternal grandfather wrote for two national evangelical publications: *The Sunday School Times* and *The Christian Herald*. He was a postal worker in New York City; and on weekends, in addition to shepherding his wife and children to church, he visited the criminally insane ward at Bellevue Hospital to preach to the prisoners. My father's brother, Uncle Rob, was a Presbyterian minister who married my mother's sister, Evelyn. They belonged to the Orthodox Presbyterian Church, a splinter group whose beliefs were rigidly and narrowly fundamental.

Uncle Rob's stature was such in the family that no disagreement was possible on complex doctrinal issues. Not until I was well past fifty and he was in failing health was I able to tell him that our beliefs did not mesh but that I would like to correspond with him anyway. I still treasured the information he, as the last living member of his generation, had stored in his head about the family. He continued to write to me in a shaky hand from the nursing home, but in each letter he lovingly admonished me about the error of my ways. He was another of those saints from my childhood, and doing whatever had to be done lovingly was a strong family trait.

My father had not aspired to teach or preach, but took the raising of his four children in the faith, his role as chairman of the deacon's board in the Baptist Church we attended, and his deep involvement in the Gideons International, a Bible distribution organization, as his primary Christian duties to be discharged with uncomplaining fervor. My mother of ten said, "Your father is a saint."

My Aunt Evie was the perfect minister's wife. She taught both children and adults in the church and gained some recognition in our family for her writing and her "flannelboard" stories. When she visited us in the summer, she would set up her flannel-covered easel in the living room and to my great delight, would begin placing a flannel-backed sweep of blue sky, marshmallow clouds, bulrushes, Gideon's ladder, the woman at the well, Christ feeding the multitude with loaves and fishes or Paul on the road to Damascus—adding pieces as the story unfolded. She also submitted "illustrations" (stories that illustrated an announced Bible text) to a weekly contest held by *The Sunday School Times*. The winners were awarded $5 for each illustration printed, and the fact that she earned money in this way enhanced her stature in my mind.

One summer Aunt Evie and I were both visiting my grandparents in Brooklyn. I was no more than six years old. As my aunt tucked me into bed one evening, her kind, loving voice took on added earnestness. "Ruthie," she asked, "do you know what will be the most important decision you will ever make in your life?" I recall to this day how badly I wanted not to disappoint her. I hesitated long and finally responded, "Is it the man I marry when I grow up?" I knew immediately it was the wrong answer. "Well, that's very important," she said, "but the most important decision is to let Jesus into your heart." She wanted to be the instrument of my conversion. She was childless while her sister, my mother, had four children ι perhaps been too busy to see to my salvation.

We knelt down by the bed, and she prayed and then gave me the right words to utter so that I could accept Jesus into my heart. There were no accompanying bells, skies opening, or heavenly revelations. I felt and acted just as I had previously, and with the wisdom of a child, I knew that I had only done this to make Aunt Evie happy. My salvation would still be self-determined with no credit given even to a favorite aunt.

My mother's life is a more painful tale to tell. While she held as precious all the prescribed beliefs of her beloved father and husband, she always felt that if she were a better Christian, if only her faith were stronger, she could conquer her fears, would not be prone to the nervousness that plagued her days. She was afraid of so many things, but at the crux of it all was the fear that she couldn't measure up to the expectations of others, even, perhaps, God. An impending meeting to attend, a trip to take, company coming for dinner—all these things preyed heavily on her mind, and she would suffer one of her "sick headaches" which many times prevented her from doing the very things she wanted to do most.

She had a lovely soprano voice and in her younger days had been a soloist. She was often asked to sing a solo at church. Because this had the added importance of being something that she could "do for the Lord," she was especially anxious to comply. It meant that at the given time on the program, she must walk down to the front of the church, nod to the accompanist, and sing. Only her family knew the reason she stood so close to the piano or organ. "If I can put one hand on it, it steadies my trembling knees," she always told us.

We drove 30 miles round trip to what my parents considered the only "sound" church in the region and spent roughly 16 hours a week attending services. This entailed two services on Sunday, the youth group on Tuesday nighs and prayer meeting on Thursday night —not an easy life for robust, energetic kids.

The adults tried to make religion palatable to children. "Sword Drill" was a favorite game we played in Sunday School. On the command, "Raise your swords," we all placed our Bibles in our right hand and raised them above our heads. This prevented cheating. The a book of the bible, chapter, and verse were announced by the adult. On the command of "Go," we rushed to find the selection in the Bible.

it and read it aloud gained a point for his team. We
.mes of the books of the Bible about the time we
.abet. Rewards were given to the child who memorized
verses or chapters. Throughout our childhood, we were
participate in various programs for reading the Bible
in ___ .ie year. My older brother, Bud, actually did this many
times, foreshadowing his outstanding ministerial career and enabling
him to recite long passages from memory.

There were also marathon missionary conferences, Daily
Vacation Bible School, summer Bible conferences and trips to hear
leading evangelists of the day speaking in New York City. Before the
day of Jerry Falwell, Jim Baker, Pat Robertson and Robert Schuller,
there was Charles Fuller in Pasadena and Percy Crawford in
Philadelphia. Jack Wyrtzen in New York City and Billy Graham were
just getting started in what later became worldwide evangelizing
ministries, which still continue today. As teenagers we traveled to hear
them speak in standing-room only crowds at Madison Square Garden
and Carnegie Hall. When I try to analyze the appeal of these wildly
popular men, I realize that they combined an aura of deep spirituality
with more than a touch of sensuality. They were physically attractive
men with magnetic personalities and stage presence. They used the
tools we now associate with show business and politics to draw and
keep their crowds.

The role of women in this fundamentalist culture was entirely
subservient. She was a "handmaiden," a "helpmate," and understood
her greatest gift to be the care of her husband and children. She was
silent in church. She could provide music, food, handiwork, altar
flowers, communion cloths and the starched robes or collars worn by
the minister. She could teach her children to love God and revere his
male representatives. It was sometimes whispered that she had
influence over the decision-making of one of these men, but this was
not an attribute to be admired or emulated.

My two older brothers, not surprisingly, chose as young men to
be ministers. This could be achieved in some churches by attending a
two-year Bible college. My brothers chose four-year liberal arts
colleges followed by three years of seminary. This was seven years out
of their young lives. After all this scholarship and the early bright days
of their ministries, they both had second thoughts. By mid-life with
wives and children dependent upon them, each with his own reasons

left the ministry. I was spared ever thinking of my brothers as saints. They were were flesh and blood, as was I.

My parents saw no reason for a daughter to attend college, since her greatest goal in life was to marry and have children. To prove the seriousness of my intentions, after high school I went to work in an insurance office. I saved enough for my first year's tuition, room and board; and with summer wages and a bond left to me by my grandparents, I entered a strictly fundamentalist college. In addition to majoring in English, I minored in Bible, providing me with more than a nodding acquaintance with the Old Testament prophets and the New Testament apostles.

Throughout my teens and during three years of college, I wholeheartedly embraced the tenets of the Christian faith handed down to me by my forefathers and mothers. While I was always shy and reluctant to give personal testimony, I tried hard to be the kind of Christian they approved. I didn't have "worldly" friends in high school. I never even had a date with a boy. I dressed modestly and only occasionally applied lipstick after I boarded the bus for high school. I didn't dance, play cards or attend the movies. I even distributed tracts intended to awaken the non-believer, not by personal confrontation but by surreptitiously leaving them in ladies rooms and other public places.

Following my junior year of college, I married a handsome member of the gospel quartet that represented the college—a choice approved by my parents. He perceived the gender roles in much the same way as my parents and grandparents. He was the head of the house; his interests both professional and recreational took precedence over mine. I had learned the subservient role and had never learned to consider my own needs and wants as legitimate, much less to claim them.

As a young married couple, we had family devotions after the evening meal. The head of the house then retired to his own pursuits— whether reading the paper, homework (for he acquired two Masters degrees during our marriage), his ham radio, a game of volleyball, basketball, tennis, golf or bowling with his colleagues, choir or Oratorio practice. His gender role included house and car repair, yard and garden work, but also included hunting and fishing with my father or buddies his own age.

My gender role was to be an unresisting bed partner, to bear the children (we had four), provide meals, keep the house clean and inviting, bathe the babies, dress the babies, get them up and put them to bed, do the family laundry, iron the breadwinner's white shirts, be kind to friends and neighbors (this often took the form of baking or cooking), and do such entertaining of children or guests as needed. No disposable diapers, dishwashers or driver's license in those early days. The good wife was too busy to wander the malls, go to exercise class, read except late at night or fritter away her time trying to write. What does she know, anyhow? And there was the rub. The good Christian fundamentalist wife held few opinions or positions of her own—she reflected the bright light of her father's/husband's wisdom.

As children grew and started school, I could pick up a book during infant nap time and before the older ones returned from school. It is impossible to overstate the power of what I read. Before the age of 35, at school, in my parent's home, at a Christian college, in my own home, I read the wisdom of white men. Suddenly then, across my path came those first bold, brave women who articulated what I knew to be true. Like the blazing sun, it had the warmth to begin a thaw in my frozen soul.

(The second and final part of this essay will appear in *Upstream 2*.)

Ruth Peterson has moved "Upstream" from her childhood home near Kingston on the Hudson, and spent much of her adult life living at the juncture of the Alplaus Creek and the Mohawk River at the spot where the French and Indians camped the night before burning Schenectady. She was a public relations professional for many years and has written Op-Ed pieces for *The Sunday Gazette* since 1993. She considers her four sons and one daughter her greatest legacy.

Tal Streeter and Public Art in the City of Amsterdam

Daniel Weaver

On Friday, August 28, 1981, the formal completion of the Amsterdam Mall, now known as the Riverfront Center, was marked with the dedication of a three-piece sculpture at the mall's west entrance on Church Street.

Amsterdam Colors by Tal Streeter

Not everyone appreciated the sculpture. It's modernity turned off people who were more attuned to traditional sculpture. In fact, when the sculpture was first unveiled, I did not care for it much either. However, once I learned more about the sculptor, my appreciation for him and his work grew.

This year marks the 30th anniversary of the sculpture, *Amsterdam Colors,* which was created by sculptor Tal Streeter. Streeter grew up in Manhattan, Kansas and graduated from the

University of Kansas with an M.F.A in design and sculpture. He taught at the University of Kansas for a while before moving to New York City to start a career in sculpture. Eventually, he would end up teaching at SUNY Purchase.

Streeter is now recognized as the first western artist to pay attention to the art of kite making, particularly Japanese kites. An understanding of Streeter's fascination with kites, makes his art easier to understand and appreciate. Streeter has traveled the globe to research kite making. He has published many articles and books about kite making, including *Domina Jalbert: Brother of the Wind*, *The Philosopher's Kite* and *A Kite Journey Through India*, the proceeds from which were used to establish a bank loan program for women in India.

The sculpture Streeter created for Amsterdam is made of tubular stainless steel. Each of the three pieces has a triangular frame that looks similar to a triangular box kite. Each of these frames was covered by different colored sailcloth when first erected. The cloth was to be replaced at regular intervals with cloth of other colors. However, the cloth wore out over time, and it has been many years since any of the pieces have been covered with cloth. The lack of sail cloth on the sculptures causes them to blend in to the background, which might explain why many residents of Amsterdam are not even aware that there is a sculpture at the west end of the Riverfront Center.

Although modern, *Amsterdam Colors* still falls into the ancient category of sculpture. While creating many physical sculptures that can be displayed and viewed over and over, Streeter eventually went beyond the traditional ideas of fine arts to become a sky artist or wind artist. In a 2003 interview with Nancy Lowden Norman prior to the Windart Kite Festival, Streeter defined sky art, wind art and kite art as "art that flies."

While wind artists or sky artists create something, and sometimes that something is a physical thing (e.g. a kite), it can be as much performance art as it is traditional art. Wind art, for example, may include kite festivals, which are a one time, non-permanent art event. On the other hand, one of Streeter's most famous sculptures, a work of sky art, *Endless Column*, is a 70 foot high red painted steel column that zig zags up into the sky. It is on permanent display at the Storm King Art Center in the Hudson Valley. Its popularity can be seen by the number of times people have posted photos of it on the internet.

Amsterdam Colors is important for two reasons. First, it was created by a world class sculptor. Secondly, when I began this essay, it was the only piece of outdoor public art in the City of Amsterdam, although Amsterdam will have another piece of public art soon. In fact it might already be installed by the time this article appears in print. The new piece of public art, *Painted Rocks of Amsterdam*, is a replica of the Native American pictographs which once were visible on rocks along the Mohawk River but no longer exist. This work will be located in the Riverlink Park, near the site of the original painted rocks. The new sculpture is also the work of a gifted sculptor, Alice Manzi.

Public art, according to Ian Chilvers, "...can in its broadest sense be applied to any painting or sculpture designed to be displayed in public open spaces but which since about 1970 has also been used in a more restricted sense to refer to art that is envisaged as part of the life of the community in which it is sited."

About some of the benefits of public art, the Newport News Public Art Foundation states, "Beyond its enriching personal benefits, public art is a true symbol of a city's maturity. It increases a community's assets and expresses a community's positive sense of identity and values. It helps green space thrive, enhances roadsides, pedestrian corridors, and community gateways; it demonstrates unquestionable civic and corporate pride in citizenship and affirms an educational environment. A city with public art is a city that thinks and feels."

Public art is not without its problems and critics. The Public Art Around the World website points out both the positive and negative sides of public art. It also collects and displays examples of public art from around the world. Some public art has been controversial, like the sculpture in northern Italy by German artist, Martin Kippenberger, of a crucified frog holding a beer and an egg. Public art in some touristy places can be tacky. Nevertheless, good public art can enhance a city's image, and controversial and even tacky public art can draw tourists.

Surely Amsterdam needs more public art, and it has many vacant public spaces where it can be created. For example the wide grassy space along the north side of the arterial cutting through Amsterdam from east to west would make a great site for public art. I can envision a long ribbon of concrete, much like a sidewalk, installed parallel to the arterial. On top of it, I can see sculptures of a long column of working people, some by themselves and some in twos and threes, walking to the mills. Working children would be represented as well. Each sculpture could be the creation of a different artist—some might be representational, some abstract.

While Amsterdam is full of war memorials, and although streets and buildings are named after the wealthy industrialists who once lived in Amsterdam, there is no memorial to the working people who built this city. An old man once told me how the streets of the city would be filled with the sound of hundreds of people walking to work in the carpet and other mills that dominated the city. He described this daily event in such a way that I could see and hear the crowds of people tramping up the hill to work.

A form of public art that has been around a long time is the mural. The murals of Diego Rivera spring immediately to mind, as well as those created through the New Deal's many art programs during the Great Depression. In many cities, the murals created during the Great Depression have been allowed to deteriorate. Amsterdam is fortunate in that it has two well cared for Treasury Department Arts Projects murals in its post office. One is of a meeting of Sir William Johnson with some native Americans. The other is an Erie Canal scene.

According to a booklet put out by the Historic Amsterdam League to accompany its historic tour during the 2011 Spring Fling, the murals were painted by H. E. Schnakenberg and completed in 1939. Schnackenberg had works on display in the Metropolitan Museum of Art, the Whitney and other galleries. He oversaw the installation of the murals which took three days. Amsterdam artist, Lucy Suhr, restored the murals in 1974.

Amsterdam, under the direction of Mayor Ann Thane, is in the process of launching an outdoor mural program. This is an exciting new venture for the city. While all the details of the program are not yet available, it would be great if some of the murals were located near downtown.

As things currently stand, Tal Streeter's *Amsterdam Colors*, Alice Manzi's *Painted Rocks of Amsterdam*, and H. E. Schnakenberg's post office murals are all within a short distance of each other. With a few more outdoor murals nearby, Amsterdam will have created a walkable art tour, which can be easily accessed by local people, tourists staying at the Best Value Inn, boaters docking at the Riverlink Park and bicyclists coming off the nearby New York State Canalway Trail.

Eventually a self-guided art, architecture and history tour could be set up, beginning on Bridge Street and ending up at the former Kellogg & Miller Linseed Oil Factory on Church Street.

Here is how I visualize the tour.

Amsterdam Castle formerly National Guard Armory. (Bed & Breakfast).
The Gray-Jewett Mansion at 80 Florida Avenue. (Private).
The Sweet Canal Store on Bridge Street. (Private).
Pedestrian Bridge over the Mohawk River.
Side trip to **Guy Park Manor/Walter Elwood Museum**. (Public).
Painted Rocks of Amsterdam sculpture.
Amsterdam Colors sculpture.
Historic Main Street.
Post Office and murals. (Public).
The Amsterdam Free Library. (Public).
The Kellogg Mansion. (Private).
City Hall and rose garden. (Public).
The Noteworthy Indian Museum. (Public).
Former Sanford Carpet Mills. (Business).
Green Hill Cemetery. (Public).
Kellogg & Miller Linseed Oil Factory. (Private).

While art is not the entire solution to revitalizing Amsterdam's downtown, it is part of the solution and is worth pursuing with a passion.

Note: After I wrote this article, work began on the first Amsterdam mural in the rose garden at city hall. See photo on next page.

Works Cited

Chilvers, Ian. "public art." *A Dictionary of Twentieth-Century Art.* 1999. Retrieved June 14, 2011 from Encyclopedia.com: http://www.encyclopedia.com/doc/1O5-publicart.html

Norman, Nancy Lowden. "An Interview With ACA WINDART Master Artist," Tal Streeter. 2003. Retrieved June 14, 2011 from *Wind Art*:
http://www.windart.subvision.net/aca-windart/sub/talstreeter/interview-aca2003.htm

"What is Public Art?" Retrieved June 14, 2011 from *Newport News Public Art Foundation*: http://nnpaf.org/what_is_art.html

Heart Of Amsterdam. Along & Near Lower Church Street. (Amsterdam, NY: Historic Amsterdam League, 2011).

Mural in progress in the rose garden at Amsterdam City Hall

Carnival

Kelly de la Rocha

It's a marvelous mosaic
from atop the Ferris Wheel.
Balloons fly, flags flap,
rides spin,
music drifts.
Too far away
to see smiles, hear laughter,
but you imagine them there
because they come with cotton candy,
are stuck to candy apples.
And everyone loves a fair, don't they?
I guess I would say
I love one, from above,
the horses like child's toys,
no dust in my throat.
Too far away to see
the chipping paint
on the funhouse railing
or smell the beer
on the carney's breath.
Too far away to see
the ant-covered lemonade cup
tossed on the ground
or the flies
around the horses' eyes.
Just far away enough
for it to look like you dreamed
it would when you were ten
and had never been.
Just far away enough to make you wish
you could look at more of life
from a rickety metal bucket
almost in the clouds.

Kelly de la Rocha is a freelance writer and editor living in Glenville. Her articles on home and garden topics frequently appear in *The Daily Gazette*. Her poetry has been featured in the *Syracuse Cultural Workers 2011 Women Artists Datebook*; in the chapbook, *Poems from 84th Street*, edited by Linda Leedy Schneider; in *Chronogram Magazine*; in *Four and Twenty's online journal*; and in Folded Word Press' e-publication, *unFold*.

~~~~~~~~~~~~~~~~

Welcome to Walmart

Todd Fabozzi

only in America
where the crowds congregate
before the rising sun
nervous for goods
anxious to shop till they drop
with itchy palms, sweaty for merchandise
in long lines, chomping at the foamy bit
ready to swipe and save
a few nickels
on a black Friday day

they elbowed and edged
crunched and punched
the mad pulse of the crushing crowd
pushing and shoving
ramming and thrusting
the doors bulged and groaned
straining to hold
the clerk yelled "no!"
as the framing let go
and the frenzied crowd flowed
in a mad desperate dash
to save a little cash
screaming and yelling

and over and over
they stomped—
thousands of ravenous feet
boot prints on his belly
stiletto heals to puncture his legs
steel tips to crush his desperate fingers
as he gasped for air not there
lying there
like a sacrificial lamb
offered to the gods of commerce
to the angels of cheap labor
to the spirits of over-consumption
who ravaged his battered body
and left him crushed dead
with hundreds of footprints
stamped on his head
and there imprinted
Made in China
it said.

Todd Fabozzi lives in Amsterdam and is an urbanist, social ecologist, writer, teacher and drummer. As a long-time advocate of sustainable design, he has lectured extensively on suburban sprawl and its consequences. He is the author of two books of poetry, which you can purchase at www.toddfabozzi.com.

~~~~~~~~~

Notable Mohawk Valley Quote

"March 4, 1884. Tuesday. Town meeting to day, but it was so very cold & windy that Hall & Hiram did not go. towards night John Sebry sent a team after H, but as he & Hall had agreed to stay at home, he did not go. Hall votes Republican & H. democrat, so if both kept at home it would be even"

Delia Denison Diary April 1883 to August 1885. The Journal of an Upstate New York Farm Wife. Galway, NY.

~~~~~~~~~

Letters to a Son at Sea

There is not much point in dwelling on the fact that letter writing is a lost art. The following letters from a self-educated General Electric employee to his son in the navy reveal what we have lost. The portions of the letters that appear here have not been edited, nor have spelling or grammar been corrected, except for a few instances in order to make the meaning clear. The spaces between the numerals of the date are the letter writer's own invention.

If you have any letters or other documents related to the Mohawk Valley that you would like to share with our readers, please let us know.

Amsterdam, N. Y.
February Twenty Ninth
1   9   4   8

Dear Marc,

...

This is the season when things in this northern clime are sort of bogged down and dull; the reaction of the holidays and the sobering effect of preparing our income statements. Saw that play The Glass Menagery at the old Erie Theatre in Schenectady. I see it has played in Rome, did you catch it in Africa? It is an unusual play, with a lot of symbolism, no definite acts but an interval in the middle of a series of scenes. It had only four actors but they were magnificent. And it was the sort of play to remember and think about ... but I don't want to think – I go to a show to laugh and be entertained with and escape from reality ... and this show ended a rather depressing note and left the audience to finish it for themselves, which was unfortunate for me as I am too much of a realist and caustic to draw anything but a tragic and morbid conclusion to such material as this plot contained. Don't fail to see it if it comes your way but don't quote me as recommending it as "entertainment".

The movies we have been getting here of late are pure tripe strait from the tripe barrel. I went to see Slave Girl and found that I had seen it before and forgotten. But I'd go to see Decarlo in Ten Nights in a Bar Room" and still enjoy watching her romp thru it. I saw

"Prince of Thieves" at the Rialto last night and it certainly was robbery. About as subtle as a sailor with a six hour pass and gaged to the I.Q. of a high school freshman. The companion picture "I Love Trouble" was of the hard-boiled-romancing-detective type that Hollywood grinds out with such drab regularity on the same repulsive pattern and makes everything perfectly confusing on the theory that if you can confuse enough people – some one will think that what you are doing is good ... and of course the guilty villan was the most innocuous and innocent character in the stinkeroo.

Amsterdam, N. Y.
May Second
1   9   4   8

Dear Marc,

...

If you have decided to retire from the Navy when your enlistment expires I think you should begin to make some plans now. If you sever your connections with the Navy you will be eligible under the G.I. bill for colledge training. This I would seriously urge you to accept. The world has advanced to the point where a colledge degree is almost a requisite for success in any but the most common jobs. We have a few men among the high brass in the G. E. who never graduated from colledge but the lines have been tightened so that when they are retired they will be replaced with colledge men. And as long as the world worships a colledge diploma the smart youth acquires one.

And the formal education that a colledge offers is not to be despised. And a self-educated man is a spottably educated man...and you are always conscious of holes and voids – like those in a swiss cheese... I don't know in what field your interests lie but electrical engineering or some allied course would seem indicated by the training you have already received. Or you may be "fed up" with that and wish to try a new field. Remember it isn't the money but the satisfaction of doing the work you like that really pays off. If you can bring some enthusiasm to your job that will net you more profit than a big salary. While you are young and have no family responsibilities try to get into that work for which you have the keenest enthusiasm.

We have been very busy in the shops – still working six days a week; but we are headed for labor trouble. The unions contract has expired and they want another round of raises which the company refuses…Well, we ought to elect a good Republican in the White House this Fall to straiten out things (?)…We had an explosion the day before yesterday in one of the laboratories that blasted a man thru the wall and hurled him to his death six stories below. I am sending you the newspaper account. One of the tradgies of science.

As ever,

Amsterdam, N. Y.
August Twenty-Nighth
1   9   5   0

Dear Marc,

Only the poet or the saint can water an asphalt pavement in the confident anticipation that lilies will reward his labors; but I do wish you could sublimate your neurotic impediment to writing an occasional letter. I've had one since the Fourth of July and John tells me he hasn't had any. Were you scarred in your youth by a pen or pencil held in the hands of an irate teacher?

Glad you have a television – that should be a lot of fun and entertainment, and you should be pretty expert, now, in manipulating and repairing the set. What make is it? …and which wrestler won? How do the politicians shape up over television? They say it takes a big statesman to come thru the hole in a television set without loosing weight.

It's a shame the way things are going in Korea. I think the people begin to see the mistake they made electing Mr. Truman. How are you making out with the reserve board?????

Amsterdam, N. Y.
Sunday Night.

Dear Marc,

Well, I guess it's my turn to apologize for not writing, but wasn't it Voltaire who said, "Never explain or apologize. Your friends don't need it…and your enemies won't believe you, anyhow". But I fear you may be again encrusted with sea salt before this reaches you and for the sake of the record – here it is. You delayed so long sending us your address. I had a nice note from your chaplain at Great Lakes informing us of you having a place among his flock about ten days or two weeks before we heard from you. And I can't work up a letter writing mood on too short notice.

The G. E. decided to suspend Saturday work through July and August. The angle is that employees draw two or three weeks vacation pay. Most of them like to take it during the summer months. The amount of pay is the average of the previous eight weeks of work prior to the vacation. So the company has figured to pay vacations on the basis of a five day work week instead of six. Which in the case of a small, struggling firm like G. E. only amounts to a saving of a million or so.

. . .

A couple of weeks ago, John and Be with the children and Henrietta and I went to the Ringling's circus in Schenectady. John drove the family down and picked me up in Schenectady, after work. We saw the side show and fed peanuts to the elephants. Only animal act outside elephants and horses and seals was some trained bears. I guess I missed most the lions and tigers snarling at the trainer with his whip and chair. A lot of the circus boys and girls only risk their necks twice a day to earn their money. We had good seats but ringside, like the wrestling show, and when they staged an elephant act in the track in frount of the stand I almost thought Jumbo was sitting on my knees.

. . .

With all our love.

As ever,

Amsterdam, N. Y.
April Twenty-Third
1 9 5 1

Dear Marc,

You certainly joined the right branch of the service. Skiing in the Alps! But did you get into the "Swiss Navy" by mistake? What a blow to John Paul Jones and his buddies. I expect to hear soon that the Navy is busting broncs and wrestling steers…Where are you now, playing golf in the Sahara?

…

The hottest news in the states this week has been McArthur. Personally he leaves me cold but he certainly received a raw deal from the Missouri miget and I'm glad to see justice done to him for his long and devoted services.

Good Luck… Take care of yourself… and keep your chin up. Love from all.

As ever,

Amsterdam, N. Y.
May Thirteenth
1   9   5   1

Dear Son,

We had a rather disturbing murder close by. You remember Percy Morley, who kept the candy and sporting goods store at the corner of Wall and Division Streets? Someone stabbed him and a friend last week and robbed the place. They are holding Thomas Mullarkey for the deed. Did you know him? He must have been going to High School about the time you were there. The story is he was fired from High School and from St. Mary's and from some school in Albany that he later attended. He must have always been a problem child. A senseless, wanton murder for forty or fifty dollars. I've known Percy all my life, he used to live directly back of the store on Lefferts Street, where I was born. A good fellow; too bad he had to be the victim of a stupid, cheap assassin.…

The McArthur is the man of the hour. The whole country is off on some sort of an emotional binge over him. If there were an election tomorrow, he could be president. And he has certainly raised an issue. He has an angle that is refreshingly positive after the procrastination of Truman, Acheson and the U.N. But it seems to me that in taking on China we will only be magnifying the Korean mess. We will pour our men and equipment out in a futile massacre of the poor, benighted, chineese when we ought to save our "Sunday punch" for Joe Stalin. Of course, the tragic mistake was Truman's abandonment of Nationalist China as you so clearly saw years ago and which Mac emphasizes.

Well – pour on the coal and get back in home waters soon. We can't provide such spectacles as Pompeii, where time was frozen in hot cinders, two thousand years ago, …but we can offer you – hot dogs and ice cream. All our love and best wishes.

As ever,

Dad

~~~~~~~~~~~~~~

Notable Mohawk Valley Quote

"For three hundred and sixty miles, gentlemen, through the entire breadth of the state of New York; through numerous populous cities and most thriving villages; through long, dismal, uninhabited swamps, and affluent, cultivated fields, unrivaled for fertility; by billiard-room and bar-room; through the holy-of-holies of great forests; on Roman arches over Indian rivers; through sun and shade; by happy hearts or broken; through all the wide contrasting scenery of those noble Mohawk counties; and especially, by rows of snow-white chapels, whose spires stand almost like mile-stones, flows one continual stream of Venetianly corrupt and often lawless life."

Herman Melville's description of the Erie Canal in *Moby Dick*.

~~~~~~~~~~~~~~

9/11 Ten Years After

It's hard to believe that it has been ten years since 9/11/01. The following two pieces deal with the aftermath of it. The first piece is a record of Amsterdam attorney Robert N. Going's days as a Red Cross volunteer in NYC. It is a powerful account of what he encountered at ground zero while experiencing a crisis of his own.

The second piece by Daniel Weaver has to do with Ward Churchill's notorious "little Eichmanns" remark following 9/11 and Hamilton College's decision to cancel his appearance there.

~~~~~~~~~~~~~~~~

Ground Zero Diary

Robert N. Going

November 2, 2001

Nearly two months have passed and the fires are still burning. When the wind shifts, as it has for the last couple of days, the air becomes heavy, eye-stinging, lung irritating and carries with it the stark reality of what happened two blocks from where I now sit.

I am spending three weeks as a Red Cross Disaster Relief Mass Care volunteer, assigned to Respite Center One within the heavily restricted combat zone. Here we provide meals and comfort to the rescue workers, technicians, security personnel, etc. around the clock in the great tradition of the Red Cross. Folks are here from all over the country pitching in.

We never know from day to day who our co-workers will be. Yesterday it was five office workers from Orlando who were in town briefly on business for the Campus Crusade for Christ. They all came in to help for one day on the midnight to 8 a.m. shift. They figured they could sleep on the plane on the way home. They were here and wanted to help, and that was that.

We are surrounded by mail, posters, drawings from school kids all over the country. Hundreds, thousands, tens of thousands, and it all gets read and rotated on a regular basis. Sit down for dinner, and there's a stack of mail waiting for you. They've even separated the ones with return addresses so that the exhausted police and firefighters can sit down and write a quick thank-you. Most of it is incredibly moving. "Out of the mouths of babes." One youngster said he thought he knew what they must feel like, because he had a cousin who died. Another, with handwriting that I would guess was no more than fourth grade, simply enclosed a comforting verse from one of the Psalms.

Hopefully it will be the gravest event of their lifetimes, perhaps even more shocking and horror-filled to them than it is for us adults who have longer memories. Yet, they all seem to have understood it, grasped instinctively the terrible evil of it all, recognized the virtues of country and family and laying down one's life for others.

I arrived Monday night. It was a pleasant night, so I walked the 18 blocks up 8th Avenue to my hotel. Around 44th Street I was startled to come upon a full-size bronze statue of a fireman kneeling in sorrow over a fire helmet. The statue was on a tow-trailer and had already become a shrine.

It seems this statue had been commissioned for some place in Missouri. By odd coincidence it was delayed at Customs when it arrived in New York on September 9th. After the 11th, all agreed it would stay in New York. Lacking a permanent location, it is simply parked in the street.

A few blocks further up there is a firehouse, covered with messages of encouragement from people who now consider themselves New Yorkers even if they've never stepped foot here. And there were the portraits of the fifteen men from that company who were killed on 9/11. Now they were not just numbers, but flesh and blood: smiling, clowning, surrounded by friends and family.

> *"We are the dead,"* the poet said.
> *Short days ago we lived, felt dawn,*
> *Saw sunset glow.*
> *Loved and were loved. . .*

And now they lie beneath the rubble where their colleagues have carried on their desperate search all these weeks. Their friends wander over to our oasis, day after day, to catch a few hours sleep (each with a teddy bear donated from who-knows-where), watch some television, get a massage or a hot meal, play video games, anything to drive away the terrible reality they face on a daily basis. Some of the

Red Cross volunteers do nothing more than sit around a table and chat. A friendly smile can cause amazing transformations.

It was a good week to be here. The three Yankee home games in the World Series gave them something to cheer about. Even I got into the act, dressing up as a Yankee fan for Halloween.

None of us know how any of this will turn out. But for now, it is enough to know that in some small way each of us can do something. As for me, I was here less than an hour before I was promoted to Third Shift Dessert Coordinator.

November 4, 2001

Yesterday while waiting with some fellow Red Cross Volunteers for the shuttle bus that would take us to our stations at Ground Zero I suddenly felt a hand on my back. I whipped around only to see man walking briskly away from me down 42nd Street. I turned around and my companions were laughing.

"Get used to it," said one of the veterans who had been here a week longer. "That was a pat on the back. It happens a lot."

Perhaps because of my exceptional skill with a bagel-cutting knife (less than a week ago, I didn't even know there WAS such a thing), I have been invited to senior staff meetings. After about your second day you're considered one of the old pros around here. Virtually the entire staff turns over every three weeks, yet things seem to run very smoothly.

There was a lot of excitement here this week, first with the "gold strike" beneath the former North Tower of the World Trade Center. The Brinks trucks were running around all night for a couple of nights. Something over 200 million dollars worth was removed.

Then a couple of days ago the terrible confrontation between the firefighters and police, not far outside our door here at Respite Center One. Emotions had been running high, naturally. Faced with the awful dilemma of the sincere and worthy desire of recovering as many of the bodies as possible and the reality of the continuing danger of the site and the risk of more casualties, the Mayor has decided to cut back dramatically on the number of firefighters digging through the rubble for their lost comrades.

In the heat of the moment, things were said and done that have caused at least for now a dreadful schism. Several firefighters were arrested after punching out several of the cops. For us, it's worse than watching two of your children fighting, especially knowing all the while that the endless stress of this work has caused otherwise reasonable people to act in uncharacteristic ways.

We Red Cross workers don't have that problem. We took a stress management class the other night.

"Tell us about some things that are causing you stress and how you deal with them."

"Well," said one of the workers, "Yesterday the bus driver kept lurching the bus around, starting and stopping. He shook me up so much I could hardly think."

"And my husband," said another "he . . ."

"Wait a minute," I said. "Isn't anybody feeling any stress from that. . .that . . .," and I pointed to the window and realized I didn't have the words to describe what had happened across the street. That, what?

Tragedy? A tragedy is when you give your dog a bowl of water and it turns out to be antifreeze. Catastrophe? Not enough. Abomination? Too tame. How about:

Horror.

That horror that lurks and dwells in the back of our minds even when back home but especially here where we are facing it, surrounded by it, absorbed in it even while we go about our business pretending it's not there. ("The jury is instructed to pay no attention to that Mastodon in the courtroom.")

Yet there it is, just the same.

Last night we made a supply run that took us directly through Ground Zero. Bill Wills, Alderman of the 4th Ward of the City of Amsterdam and a pretty articulate guy, could find no words to describe what he saw when he returned from a trip there a few weeks ago. Neither can I.

For now, two large sections of the North Tower still stand, leaning toward a neighboring building. The fires burn. One of the steel workers told us that some of the steel is still red hot, over 1200 degrees. One adjacent building still standing has a whole side blown off, and you can see offices and file cabinets and desks and computer terminals all neatly in place. The area where the firefighters used to gather is now largely empty. It is almost inconceivable that any more bodies will be recovered in any recognizable fashion.

Earlier in the day, passing through Grand Central Station, I passed one of the many memorial kiosks that have sprung up everywhere where families could post photos of their missing. I tried to read them all, trying to make these strangers come alive at least in my heart, but there were so, so many and it doesn't take long before your eyes just get too blurry to continue.

There was a single poster of the police officers who were killed, including one female, Moira Smith. Next to her picture was posted a long letter from a man who had met her on the way out of the World Trade Center, telling of her coolness and bravery and how she had personally saved him by looking him square in the eye and telling him firmly and authoritatively which way to go and to exit the building promptly. She saved hundreds, maybe thousands of lives by doing her job in a professional manner. It's likely she wouldn't have expected anyone's thanks.

All in a day's work.

I continue to read the mail from the school kids from across the continent. Today one had written, "Yea, though I walk through the valley of the shadow of death, I shall fear no evil."

I have now driven a Red Cross Emergency Response Vehicle through the valley of the shadow of death that was once the World Trade Center, and I have seen the face of evil.

November 5, 2001

Whenever I take the subway from midtown to my Red Cross assignment at Respite Center One, Ground Zero, I continue to be drawn to "New York's Wailing Wall" at Grand Central Station where families of the missing from the World Trade Center have posted heart-breaking requests for any information. Tonight I approached just as a young woman burst into tears.

"Oh my God! That's a girl I went to school with!"

And I quickly moved on.

My immediate supervisors, a husband and wife team from North Carolina, had Saturday night/Sunday morning off. Being acclimated to the third shift, they made a late, late night of it in the city that doesn't sleep.

Suzanne is a bouncy, friendly, delightful woman. When the night was petering out, a time "when the street belongs to the cop and the janitor with the mop," as Frank Loesser would say, a hollow man approached her.

"I know why I'm out this late," he said, "but why are you?"

So she explained what we are doing, and then he told his story.

He is a former cop who had taken a job as private security and driver for an executive at the Cantor Fitzgerald firm. He was in their World Trade Center office every day, except one. On September 11, they got a late start because they had to drive the executive's son to kindergarten. Virtually the entire company went down with the tower.

Can you imagine? Everyone you work with gone at once? I thought of Robert E. Lee riding through the field on the third day at Gettysburg and coming across one of his commanders wandering aimlessly.

"General Pickett!" he admonished, "You must tend to your Division!"

"General Lee, I have no Division."

Suzanne stopped being bouncy when she told me the story. "I try to stay happy and forgot about all that, but you can't." They go home tomorrow. The Red Cross wisely sets time limits for their volunteers to prevent burn-out.

Today there was another memorial service for a firefighter at St. Patrick's. There is an altar in the church converted to a victim shrine. It gets a lot of attention.

On Sundays Catholic Mass is celebrated at Ground Zero, beneath an unusual icon. Discovered in the rubble, standing erect, rescue workers found a perfectly formed steel cross, and immediately rallied to it as a symbol of Hope. It stands at the front of the site in solemn defiance of all that is surrounding it. Many look upon it as a miracle.

I actually met the man who found it. He was introduced to me by the Fire Department Chaplain, Father Brian Jordan. Frank Silecchia is a huge, gentle man with hands three times the size of mine. Born in Brooklyn of a Jewish mother and a Roman Catholic father, he is a simple man with native eloquence and Faith to move mountains. We stood in the muck and mire midst the spirits of shattered dreams between the cross and the remains of the North Tower as he told me his tale.

Many of the buildings surrounding the World Trade Center had been crushed by the falling debris. In the hours and days following the massacre, rescue workers risked their own lives in the desperate hunt for survivors. This brought Frankie into one of those tottering shells, the Customs House, Building 6. Eventually he reached the basement, and there, in the center of the building, was a crater, and rising up out of the crater the steel cross, fully erect.

It was the morning of the third day. For twenty minutes he stood there, and wept.

It had been part of the North Tower, and as that structure came down, this cross had passed through the roof of the building, plummeted through floor after floor after floor, down, down, down until finally coming to rest where he found it.

"This is holy ground we are walking on," he told me. "All those people that died here, they're still here in a way. Don't you see?" and here he looked up to where the tower once stood. "Don't you see? Jesus was raised up on the cross, He died, and He descended to the dead. Then He gathered them up, and then," and now he turned to where his Cross stood witness, high over the widening pit, "then . . . Resurrection! And He rises and takes everyone with Him to the Father!"

Father Jordan, who was still with us, nodded, and it is hard to imagine a thousand volumes of theology and philosophy that could have explained things any better.

Still, to call this a miracle is ridiculous, of course. This can be no more an act of God than the '69 Mets. Both towers and the other destroyed structures had steel frames and doubtless thousands of such right-angle joints as might form what looks to us to be a cross. Right?

But symbols, which are all man-made, can nonetheless be powerful. What is the Liberty Bell other than an old decrepit piece of junk, or the tattered flag of Fort McHenry that we spend millions to preserve, or that Lady in the Harbor? But does not each in turn stir something in
the soul?

For the Christian, the Cross is the ultimate symbol of triumph over Evil and Death. Secularly, when used by the Red Cross it becomes a symbol of Hope and Healing. Our long tradition of burying the dead under crosses goes beyond the principles of the Christian religion. True, there have been times when the cross has been usurped for ignoble causes, but here at the Gates of Hell there can be no doubt of its purpose.

Understandably, some will object to such a prominent display of religion in a public place.

But if, on a crisp autumn day when the pipes play "Amazing Grace" and the drum sounds the Dead March, some widow or child or mom or dad glances up at that cross and thinks for but a moment, "I am the Resurrection and the Life," who among us should say them nay?

November 11, 2001

"Thanks," said the President of the United States as he shook my hand and looked me square in the eye after the international memorial service at Ground Zero on Sunday. Moments later Governor Pataki and Mayor Giuliani came by as well. Rudy signed my hard-hat.

It's nice to feel appreciated, finishing up my second week as a Red Cross Disaster Relief volunteer at Ground Zero in New York City. It was not the first thanks I had gotten that day. The first was a general thanks to the relief workers in a letter from a sixth grade girl in South Carolina. She had sent along a lucky penny to help us out, so I sent one back to her

Then there was the thanks received from a police sergeant. A couple of us had sat with him at a dinner table in Respite Center One and listened.

"For the first couple of weeks, I just couldn't come down here," he said.

Stationed in the Bronx, on September 11 he was running an errand downtown. He saw the second plane hit, saw the flaming jet fuel incinerating everything in its path, saw bodies hurtling through the air, saw people jump, saw the whole thing come crumbling down.

"I hope you've worked through it," offered companion.

"Yeah, I'm o.k. with it now."

Right.

He is in charge of one of the security checkpoints. Says it's much better than duty at the Staten Island landfill, where the remains of the World Trade Center are sifted for body parts. Piece by piece, the rubble rides across a conveyor belt where workers using garden tools look for anything that might contain the DNA of a former human being, tossing same into buckets for later more detailed analysis.

So many stories. One of our regular volunteers is a 19 year old drama student with the singing voice of an angel, who comes down here to work the midnight to eight shift then runs cheerfully off to class. The school is in the upper west side of Manhattan. All phone service and public transportation were halted on September 11. A young man she knew was unable to contact his girlfriend, who was either in or near the World Trade Center. He borrowed a pair of roller blades and glided five miles to search for her (he found her safe and sound.)

Before the President arrived I attended Mass beneath the steel cross at Ground Zero. We threw some scrap lumber down in the mud and laid some sheets of plywood over it and that was our sanctuary. The heavy machinery shut down out of respect. OSHA regulations notwithstanding, we uncovered our heads. At the remembrance section we were asked to call out the names of those who had died. There were many. So many Irish firemen it almost sounded like a reading of the Dublin white pages. The only hymn was "God Bless America", echoing unevenly off the burned out hulk of the World Trade Center.

It was Veterans' Day, and for that we gave thanks as well.

November 12, 2001

After working the midnight to eight shift, I had just settled into my pillow when the phone rang.

"Are you watching television?" asked my wife. "Another plane went down."

I tried to focus and tuned in on the early confused reports but the unmistakeable rising smoke from Queens on an otherwise brilliantly clear day.

I was awake.

The phone lines to Red Cross headquarters in Brooklyn were all tied up. I decided to try to get there and see if I could help.

The Secret Service Agents guarding my floor were all pacing (they were protecting my floor neighbor, the president of the Congo). Outside on 42nd street an emergency traffic lane had been set up. Police were everywhere.

After determining the subways were still running, I dashed the three long blocks to Grand Central Station (not exactly ready for the

Amsterdam High School Cross Country team, but I did pretty good), jumped on the train downtown and switched to the A-train to Brooklyn. Two young men stopped me to ask what I knew. They both lived in the Rockaway section of Queens, where the plane went down. I knew nothing.

At Headquarters they had me stand by. I wandered about the control room and was amazed at the efficiency of the operation. They already had a command center set up at JFK airport, two emergency response vehicles on the scene, accurate maps printed out of the crash site together with specific directions for getting there. Six more fully-manned vehicles were at the command center. One man on the telephone was clearly and professionally gathering information and repeating same.

When he hung up the phone he said very calmly, "Just so you are aware, they anticipate no survivors." And then, he swallowed hard and looked away.

A lot of arm-chair quarterbacks have been criticizing the Red Cross lately. Personally, I have been tremendously impressed by everything I've seen.

I was released and went back to my hotel.

November 19, 2001

Twenty-four hours a day a spot just outside the entrance to the Ground Zero work site is occupied by a changing but dedicated bunch whose sole function is to cheer and wave when rescue and relief workers enter or leave. Over at the morgue another group continuously recites Jewish prayers for the dead, and will do so until all the thousands of body parts recovered receive a proper burial. It seems everyone wants to do something.

We have quite a mix of folks volunteering here at Respite Center One at Ground Zero in New York City, where I am in my third and final week as a Red Cross volunteer. The core group on the midnight to 8 shift are three-weekers from around the country: North Carolina, Tennessee, Michigan, Indiana, Louisiana, California, Alaska, Washington State, even one from Canada.

Supplementing these are "local" volunteers, who are not necessarily from New York, who come in for a night or several or never leave. There are students and actors, lawyers, accountants, office workers, retired folks, etc. One night we had a lady cutting bagels who had been on *As the World Turns* for fourteen years. Many people stay all night and then leave to go to work. All are cheerful and wonderful.

This being a cosmopolitan city, there are occasional communication difficulties.

"Y'all know whut ah caint stan?" commented a spitfire from Nashville, "Et's these furren buhs drav-vers. Thy tok so funny, somtams ah caint unnerstan a WURD thy sigh, y'all know whutah maine?"

Yes, I think I do.

Then there's Vikki.

Vikki is a "local" volunteer from Yorkshire, England, very near my wife's ancestral village. She is a policewoman there and was so taken by the events here that she dropped everything and flew to New York at her own expense and has been staying at the YWCA and coming in night after night to volunteer. If that isn't enough, before she left home she obtained an ankle tatoo of the Stars and Stripes intertwined with the Union Jack with the legend "God Bless America."

The other day she went shopping at a police uniform and paraphernalia store. Her speech betrayed her to an off-duty police officer. "You're Vikki, aren't you?" he asked. Upon ascertaining his honorable intentions, she permitted him to continue. "We've been looking for you. We heard all about you and want to do something to say thanks."

So the NYPD PBA set her up in a nice hotel room in midtown Manhattan for the duration of her stay.

Things are winding down here for our operation, and with each passing day more of our national folks are going home. As one of the principal Emergency Response Vehicle operators, it generally falls upon me to take them on a final tour of the Ground Zero area. One of the last stops is a pair of impromptu memorials. One we call the "Teddy Bear Site", where friends and relatives of the September 11 victims have left flowers, messages, and hundreds of stuffed animals. Across the walkway, ironically near a permanent memorial to police killed in action in New York, is a site dedicated to the various police agency and fire department personnel lost on that fateful day.

Among the many messages is a letter written to FDNY Captain Thomas Farino:

To Daddy
I love you more than forever.
I am glad for two reasons. One reason is that I am happy God is making you happy.
Also my second reason is that you died in a very honorable way and the world thinks and is thankful that you saved people and you are a hero.
Thank you Dad.

In the last twenty-four hours the bodies of at least twelve firefighters have been removed from the rubble of the North Tower of the World Trade Center. This has coincided with the most spectacular Leonid meteor showers of our lifetime.

The heavens themselves blaze forth the death of princes.

One cannot come to this place without being changed, and changed utterly.

November 24, 2001

"So you're a judge, are you?" inquired Vikki from Yorkshire after reading the article I had written about her activities as a Red Cross Volunteer in the *Amsterdam Recorder*. "That's funny. I had you pegged for a construction worker."

It is my last day after nearly four weeks at Respite Center One at Ground Zero in New York City. In some ways it is the most difficult.

"Just what exactly is the circulation of the *Recorder*," she asked.

"I'm not sure precisely," says I, "but I do know that the combined circulation of the *Recorder* and the *Reader's Digest* is something over 22 million." She was impressed.

Mary and the younger two children have spent most of the week with me and together we have witnessed this great city returning to some normalcy: the Macy's parade, the Radio City Music Hall Christmas show, lines around the block waiting to get into the brand new *Toys R Us,* the two hour wait to get into the Empire State Building Observation Deck. Of course, we couldn't help but notice that at any given moment about three quarters of the crowd were facing south, pointing in the direction of what once was. We went at twilight, and saw the effect of the gazillion watts of light being turned on at what had been the World Trade Center.

When Ronald Reagan was in the Army film office during the war, he came into possession of the footage of the U.S. Army liberating the Nazi death camps. He kept a copy for himself and showed this horror to his two sons on their respective twelfth birthdays. He wanted them to learn the possibilities of evil, of man's inhumanity to man, and to make sure they would never forget.

On Wednesday I took my family for a long walk around the periphery of Ground Zero so they could see for themselves, showed them the police and fire memorials, and the Teddy Bears. We took our time, reading as many of the tributes as were still legible, soaking in the wedding pictures, the printed church services, the decaying flowers, the birthday gifts come too late, the thousands of goodbyes.

On Friday my oldest child, Anna, came down with her college roommate. They worked with me here at the Respite Center on my last night. I took them to the same places, and drove them through the valley of the shadow of death. That will be my last memory of this place.

Calvin Coolidge said that each of us should strive to live our lives in such a way that we become the hero of our own life's story. I have seen plenty of people doing that down here. And it truly is a great feeling to get notes from your kids addressed, "My Dad, the Hero."

But I'm no hero, and I know that. I'm only here to make a small down payment on an old debt.

My father was in the Normandy campaign in the Second World War, and his father and uncle in World War I. My great-great grandfather was in the Army of Northern Virginia and survived Pickett's Charge at Gettysburg.

I'll never forget the day my older brother Jay came home from the Army and announced at the dining room table, jauntily, "Well, I nailed the plum assignment. I'm going to Vietnam." Our father's face beamed with pride, masking his fear; our mother's face full of fear, masking her pride. They were, of course, of a different and most remarkable generation.

But I fought the Battle of Albany State, supporting our troops without being one, waving the flag in the face of protestors, insisting on taking exams when others demanded the university be shut down.

Mine was the last year for automatic student deferments. The draft lottery was instituted, and I pulled a high, safe number. The war in Vietnam ended half way through my senior year and the draft abolished for good about two weeks after I graduated.

By then there was nothing left to fight for. Morale in the military began a steady decline. Our people were booed when they came home. Our fortitude was put in mothballs.

By the time pride had been restored, I had a young family and a career. The opportunity to serve had passed, and as the years flew by I advanced and became settled in my ways until one day I realized that I had become one of those gentlemen Shakespeare's *Henry V* speaks of who "think themselves accursed" and "hold their manhoods cheap whiles any speak that fought. . ."

That is why I am here, now, because it is all I could think to do.

Some final thoughts. It will be hard to imagine any problem arising that would not pale next to the destruction I have seen here. I do not see myself wallowing in self-pity any time soon. Whatever I have to face is as nothing now. This is one terrific country and its people magnificent. More and more I have become convinced of the simple truths expressed so well by Mr. Greenwood:

> *If tomorrow all the things were gone I'd worked for*
> *all my life,*
> *And I had to start again with just my children and my*
> *wife,*
> *I'd thank my lucky stars to be living here today,*
> *'Cause the flag still stands for freedom and they*
> *can't take that away!*

Epilogue

Prophecy is a funny business. The warning of the prophet only becomes obvious after the fact, they say. And so it was that less than twenty-four hours after writing those last lines, the Court of Appeals spoke. Suddenly, just after coming home, "all the things were gone I'd worked for all my life, and I had to start again with just my children and my wife."

But that's ok. After nearly four weeks at Ground Zero I realized that there are far worse fates than not being the Family Court Judge of Montgomery County.

We all had to undergo a mental health debriefing before being discharged. My worker said to me, quietly, "Tell me, how do you think you'll be able to go back and listen to the petty squabbles in Family Court after you've been here?"

I thought about it. "I'm not sure that I can."

Well. I'll never have to worry about that decision.

While riding the subway one day, I sat across from an extended family, consisting of a large black woman, her slightly retarded son in his early twenties, his sister, slightly older, and her boyfriend, a scrawny, swarthy fellow of uncertain ethnic extraction, perhaps native to anywhere from Morocco to Burma.

The son gave me a knowing look and tilted his head toward his sister's boyfriend.

"That's Osama bin Laden," he announced.

Pretty soon his mother and sister were whacking him affectionately.

"He's NOT Osama bin Laden!" the sister insisted.

"Don't pay any attention to him!" the mother warned me.

"Osama" was laughing. They were all laughing. I was laughing. Soon we were all chattering away.

New York has changed. We have all changed. A year earlier and everyone on that subway train would have been staring straight ahead. Now people talk, people laugh, people share. We are one.

Visiting firemen from Canada enter our car and people leap to offer their seats. A woman sees my Red Cross vest and follows me off the train to thank me and thank me again for being there.

I don't know how long it will last. I don't know what it all means. I leave it to the historians and the politicians and the experts to sort it all out.

But I do know this: something happened as a result of September 11.

And it is wonderful.

Robert N. Going is an attorney from Amsterdam. He is the author of two books, *The Judge Report* and *The Evil Has Landed*. Check out his books and blog at www.rgoing.livejournal.com.

Fox News In The Hen House:
Hamilton College, Ward Churchill,
9/11 and Bill O'Reilly Revisited

Daniel Weaver

The furor started in 2005 at Hamilton College in Clinton, New York. The college had invited Ward Churchill, then a professor at the University of Colorado, author, and one of the most outspoken Native American activists in North America, to be one of the speakers on a Panel Discussion on Limits of Dissent. Before the event took place, however, someone at the college discovered an essay, *"Some People Push Back": On the Justice of Roosting Chickens,* that Churchill had published on the internet on September 12, 2001 in which he used the phrase "little Eichmanns" in reference to those who worked at the World Trade Center.

While Churchill's essay had been on the internet for four years, (and was expanded into a 309 page book, *On the Justice of Roosting Chickens: Reflections on the Consequences of U. S. Imperial Arrogance and Criminality,* published in 2003), few people knew about it or had heard of Ward Churchill. That all changed when Bill O'Reilly got wind of the essay and then spun it for all it was worth in his "no spin zone."

O'Reilly attacked both Churchill and Hamilton College. He suggested that alumni withhold donations to the college unless it canceled Churchill's appearance. He even gave out the president of the college's phone number and email address. Hours after O'Reilly broke the story, Churchill had become a household word and was the lead story in the news, talk shows and on the internet for several days.

Initially Hamilton College supported Churchill's appearance, in spite of hundreds of angry emails demanding that the college cancel his appearance. Less than two weeks later, however, on February 1, 2005, the college changed its mind and canceled the Panel Discussion on Limits of Dissent, thus signifying that Churchill's dissent of American policy in the Middle East should be limited while Bill O'Reilly's dissent of Professor Churchill should not be limited. Ironically, a short time later, O'Reilly who said Hamilton should not let Churchill speak, aired a taped interview with Churchill on his program.

Hamilton College's press release of February 1, 2005, 11 AM was also ironic, so much so that I quote it here in full.

"Cancellation of Panel Discussion on Limits of Dissent

We have done our best to protect what we hold most dear, the right to speak, think and study freely.

But there is a higher responsibility that this institution carries, and that is the safety and security of our students, faculty, staff and the community in which we live.

Credible threats of violence have been directed at the College and members of the panel. These threats have been turned over to the police.

Based on the information available, I have made the decision to cancel this event in the interest of protecting those at risk.

Joan Hinde Stewart
President"

Did the college ask those at risk if they wanted to cancel the panel? And who was at risk? Primarily Ward Churchill, who was willing to appear anyway wearing a bulletproof vest and with bodyguards. No one else was forced to attend the panel. And were the threats as serious as Stewart says, or were they just a convenient excuse for canceling the panel?

But even if the threats were serious, could not security have been beefed up as Richard Cohen, no friend of Churchill, argued in a *Washington Post* column on February 5, 2005. "Hire some guards. Frisk the audience. But don't cave to the mob." Surely Cohen was right, but President Stewart made it clear that safety and security were more important than the right to speak, think and study freely. One hopes she never has to move to New Hampshire and attach that "live free or die" plate to her car.

Since the attacks of 9/11, "safety and security" have been used by all kinds of leaders to curtail civil liberties. In his 9/12 essay Churchill predicted this would happen. He said:

> "The FBI and "cooperating agencies" can be thus relied upon to set about "protecting freedom" by destroying whatever rights and liberties were left to U.S. citizens before September 11 (in fact, they've already received authorization to begin). Sheeplike, the great majority of Americans can also be counted upon to bleat their approval…"

In other places and other times, colleges and other organizations have faced the same temptation to back down when those who hate free speech have threatened them, and they have decided that free speech is equal to or more important than safety and security. Let me cite just one example, and the only reason I choose this example is I just finished reading *Peekskill: USA* by Howard Fast.

In 1949 a group of people invited Paul Robeson to sing in Peekskill, in the Hudson Valley. It was not the first time Robeson had been invited to sing there. In fact, he had already sung there three years in a row. But this time was different because some extemporaneous remarks Robeson had made, while on a recent concert tour of Europe, were garbled by the Associated Press so that they made Robeson say that Blacks would fight along side of the Soviet Union, when he actually said they would not wage war on the Soviet Union. The reaction to Robeson's misquoted remarks was the same as the reaction to Churchill's remarks, except that Walter Winchell led the attack instead of Bill O'Reilly.

So a large group of people, red neck hooligans along with prosperous middle class businessmen, blockaded the entryway to the park in Peekskill where Robeson was to sing, burned a cross and began beating hell out of the people who had already arrived. None of the concert leaders had arrived yet, so Fast quickly formed a defense committee, which proceeded to give back as good as they were getting, even though they were outnumbered. When the police arrived, they sided with the hooligans and businessmen, according to Fast, although police reports dispute this. No one died that night, but there were hundreds of injuries.

Instead of capitulating, the concert committee that Fast was part of decided to hold the concert on another night. When the concert took place, a group of men, who believed that the freedoms of speech and assembly were more important than safety and security, formed a human shield in front of Robeson, after it was discovered there were two men up on a wooded hillside with rifles aimed at Robeson.

When the concert ended, a gang of men proceeded to throw rocks and smash the windows of cars as they were leaving, injuring many of the occupants. Again, the police did not intervene, according to Fast, accept to beat some of the concertgoers themselves and arrest some as troublemakers.

Governor Thomas Dewey ordered an investigation into the incidents. Fast claimed the investigation was a whitewash. Whether Fast was right or not, the statement Dewey issued on September 14, 1949, forms an interesting contrast with that of Hamilton College President Stewart in 2005. Dewey said:

> "Two of the great cornerstones of liberty in America are freedom of assembly and freedom of speech. Without them there is no genuine liberty and these rights are guaranteed by the Constitution even to those who would destroy them. Any violation of the rights of free speech and assembly of one group is an injury to the rights of all." (Dewey, 625)

Later in his statement, Dewey said, "Free speech and the right of assembly are as precious to us as life itself." (Dewey, 626)

Governor Dewey hated Communists and "fellow travelers," yet he stated clearly that the right to free speech was theirs. He also stated that the right to free speech and assembly were as precious as life itself. He never once said that safety and security were a higher responsibility. In fact, knowing there might be trouble, he dispatched extra troopers to the scene to protect free speech, the right to assemble and the security and safety of the participants and protesters.

We should also compare Governor Dewey's response to the Peekskill affair with the response of Governor George Pataki to the appearance of Ward Churchill at Hamilton College. He said, "Let him speak. Let him say his hatred, spew his hatred, let him put out his

support for terrorism, but not at a respected forum here in New York."
(Zahn)

Few people who condemned Churchill bothered to read the full essay or the 309 page expanded version. While I don't agree with everything that Churchill said, the phrase "little Eichmanns" while sounding horrible by itself, does not sound nearly as bad when read in context. Maybe, he could have chosen a better analogy, however, his essay was written as an immediate response to what happened on 9/11, and he had little time for reflection or revision as the publisher wanted it as quickly as possible.

The images that Eichmann conjures up are those of gas chambers and crematoria. But Eichmann never directly killed any of the millions who died in the Holocaust, although the prosecution at his trial wasted a lot of time trying and failing to prove he had killed one boy with his bare hands.

Neither was he the architect of the Holocaust, as has been claimed by those who oppose Churchill. The architect of the Holocaust was none other than Hitler. Eichmann was, however, the mid-level model bureaucrat whose efficiency and organization made the Holocaust possible, a view of Eichmann similar to the one that Hannah Arendt presented in *Eichmann in Jerusalem: A Report On The Banality Of Evil*.

That's not to minimize Eichmann's role in the Holocaust, which was a large and egregious one, for which the Israelis executed him. However, the Holocaust would have still happened if Eichmann had never been born. It would not have happened if Hitler had never been born.

As Hannah Arendt wrote about Eichmann, "Certainly he had not been as big as Mr. Hausner [Israeli prosecutor] tried to make him; after all, he was not Hitler, nor, for that matter, could he compare himself in importance, as far as the "solution" of the Jewish question was concerned, with Muller, or Heydrich, or Himmler; he was no megalomaniac. But neither was he as small as the defense wished him to be" (Arendt, 57).

When Churchill called those working in the World Trade Center—not the janitors, cafeteria help or even the emergency personnel who came to rescue people from the burning towers—"little Eichmanns," he was saying that they were model bureaucrats whose financial dealings brought suffering and even death to people in developing nations, specifically Iraq. The attacks on the Pentagon and World Trade Center, he argued, were in direct response to America's destructive polices in the Middle East.

You don't have to agree with what Churchill said, but when you read the essay you realize that what Bill O'Reilly on the right, Alan Dershowitz on the left, the media and other flag draped talk show hosts said was not what Churchill actually said. And unless you are un-American, you have to admit he had the right to say it.

The Churchill saga did not end with Hamilton's cancellation of his appearance. It is still ongoing. Unable to fire Churchill from the University of Colorado because of his beliefs, the administration began to dig deeply into Churchill's writings, which are numerous, to find another reason to fire him, and they found it, as they would have in almost any professor. Churchill was guilty of the greatest crime you can commit on a college campus today, other than hate speech—plagiarism.

It's beyond the scope of this essay to deal with Churchill's alleged plagiarism. Others have already done a good job debating and debunking it. In 2007, the University fired Churchill for plagiarism. He sued the University and won in 2009. A few months later a judge overturned the jury verdict, however, stating that the University had quasi-judicial immunity and did not have to rehire Churchill. In January 2011, Churchill went back to court to appeal the judge's decision, which he is still waiting to hear.

I do not condone everything Churchill says in his essay or elsewhere. I believe that his opposition to Israel and support of the Palestinians is unbalanced. While I agree with his belief that what happened to Native Americans during most of America's history was genocide—the very word used by historian Samuel Eliot Morison who was not known for being a radical—his attempts to stop people from celebrating Columbus Day are not only ludicrous but put him in the same category as those who would deny him free speech.

While it might be possible that the government should not recognize Columbus Day as a holiday, the average American who has the day off couldn't care less about Columbus. Even Italian-Americans who celebrate it with pasta, wine and bocce are not celebrating Columbus. They are simply reveling in their heritage.

Churchill did, however, say some things in his essay that needed to be said, particularly about the arrogance of America's foreign policy, which is the central theme of his expanded essay. And in spite of Churchill's weaknesses, his radical politics and the smears against his reputation, he remains an authority on Native American culture and history.

Many white people appear to have the attitude that Indians just need to get over what happened to them. But, as Churchill points out, what happened to Native Americans in the past is still happening. By that he doesn't mean that Whites are slaughtering Indians like they used to. But to just cite just one fact, Native American males have a life expectancy of 50 years, which is only 2/3 that of white males. In his writings and lectures, Churchill shows how our past policies toward Indians are at the root of the many problems Native Americans face today.

Hamilton College, located in the heart of Iroquois country and just down the road from a former Brothertown Indian encampment in Deansboro, seems like an ideal setting for Ward Churchill to speak. Ten years after 9/11 and Churchill's infamous essay, it's time Hamilton College offered Churchill the opportunity to speak. Other colleges have done it. There have been protests, but no violence. Hamilton needs to invite Churchill, not so much because Churchill needs to speak there but because Hamilton College needs to redeem its broken pledge to protect what it claims to hold dear—"the right to speak, think and study freely."

Works Cited

http://www.hamilton.edu/news/story/college-issues-statement-concerning-churchill-visit

Arendt, Hannah. *Eichmann In Jerusalem. A Report On The Banality of Evil*. NY, NY: Penguin Books, 1985.

Churchill, Ward. "Some People Push Back": On the Justice of Roosting Chickens. September 12, 2001. Retrieved from http://www.kersplebedeb.com/mystuff/s11/churchill.html on February 21, 2011.

Cohen, Richard. "Giving Into the Mob." *The Washington Post*, February 3, 2005, Page A27. Retrieved from http://www.washingtonpost.com/wp-dyn/articles/A59185-2005Feb2.html on February 21, 2011.

Dewey, Thomas. *Public Papers of Thomas E. Dewey Fifty-first Governor of the State of New York*, pp 606-627.

Fast, Howard. *Peekskill: USA. A Personal Experience.* Moscow: Foreign Languages Publishing House, 1954

Mandel, Ian. "Controversial speaker to visit Hall." *The Spectator.* Vol. XXXXV. Number 14. January 21, 2005. Clinton, NY: Hamilton College.

Zahn, Paula. "Interview With Ward Churchill." *Paula Zahn Now.* Aired February 4, 2005 – 20:00 E.T. Transcript retrieved on February 21, 2011.
http://transcripts.cnn.com/TRANSCRIPTS/0502/04/pzn.01.html

Daniel Weaver is the Editor of *Upstream* and the owner of The Book Hound, a used and antiquarian bookstore in Amsterdam. He is also a regular contributor to the *Sunday Gazette's* op-ed page.

~~~~~~~~~~~~~~~~~~~

Notable Mohawk Valley Quote

"In eighteen ninetytwo when Eichemeyer sold out to the corporation that was to form General Electric, Steinmetz was entered in the contract along with other valuable apparatus. All his life Steinmetz was a piece of apparatus belonging to General Electric. First his laboratory was at Lynn, then it was moved and the little hunchback with it to Schenectady, the electric city.

General Electric humored him, let him be a socialist, let him keep a greenhouseful of cactuses lit up by mercury lights, let him have alligators, talking crows and a gila monster for pets and the publicity department talked up the wizard, the medicine man who knew the symbols that opened up the doors of Ali Baba's cave."

From *The 42nd Parallel* by John Dos Passos.

The Triumph of Wikileaks

L. D. Davidson

The release of purloined documents by Wikileaks, authorized by its founder Julian Assange, flushes to the surface the issue of the institutional right to hide self-designated "confidential" information from the public. As of mid-2011, it appears that Wikileaks may indeed be on the path to becoming a new public resource to combat corruption and patronage networks.

The Wikileaks organization operates on several assumptions, none of which are in any way unreasonable. First, Wikileaks apparently believes that circles of patronage within institutions are a major source of corruption in the worldwide economy. These circles of patronage function like legal gangs that serve, first and foremost, small cliques of insiders in banking, in government and in private and public corporations. The best example of this patronage problem is the chicanery that went on within companies such as Goldman Sachs, Merrill Lynch, Moody's, Lehman Brothers, Countrywide, etc. in the years leading up to the financial crisis of 2007-2011. The revolving door between the leadership of these financial service companies and the regulatory arms of the U.S. government is the best illustration of the need for organizations such as Wikileaks, whose mission is to expose to public scrutiny those small cliques of insiders who betray the spirit of laws and regulations for their own selfish benefit. A huge patronage problem does indeed exist. Wikileaks is absolutely correct on this score.

Second, Wikileaks apparently believes that the current regulatory processes are not functioning adequately to protect the public interest. Absolutely right again. In the past ten years we have observed the ease with which intra-governmental agencies such as the SEC and the EPA, not to mention the Food and Drug Administration and the IRS can be thwarted in their mandate to enforce fair and legal regulations. Whether it is a matter of enforcing drilling regulations in the Gulf of Mexico, policing unethical practices on Wall Street or enforcing straightforward tax laws, the regulatory authorities have provided inadequate oversight. The naïve idea that private corporations or government will perform adequate self-regulation has also been exposed as a sham excuse used in the self-interest of de-regulation advocates. Self-regulation simply doesn't work well. The financial crisis of 2008-2011 illustrates its limitations. The relevant question is "Who regulates the regulators"?

Third, Wikileaks apparently operates on the assumption governments and economic institutions have absolutely NO right to withhold secrets about their activities from a truly free people. Right again. All the blathering about justified government secrecy rests on the view that the temporary safety of a few hundred secret government operatives in foreign countries is more important than the permanent interests of hundreds of millions of citizens who have an interest in living in a world in which the activities of all institutions are open to public scrutiny. Governments generally know anyway about the activities of their enemies. They even possess much specific information about their military and technological capabilities. Usually it is only the general public that is left in the dark. For instance, all informed people--especially in the Iranian government--know that the western governments are trying to use cyber-weapons to thwart the dangerous Iranian nuclear program. No good reason exists for the attempt to be covert about doing such a thing. Very, very few specific details of government activities need to be in any way hidden from view. What about specific plans about airport security? But a clever security system would change its patterns in such an irregular way that the actual details of the best security plans are not fixed in time anyway. Thus, a good, hour to hour plan would not be predictable. What about the secrecy of Social Security numbers? But aren't most of them already out there in the cyber ether anyway?

How many activities are there that a responsible and just government should be hiding from their own citizens? And since when do private enterprises such as banks and insurance companies have a vested right to withhold secrets from a public whose own privacy they are already violating by the routine sale of their clients' private information to mass marketers? How so? Under what provisions of a fair constitution do financial institutions and insurance companies have the privilege to protect information about their own activities from public scrutiny? Is there some kind of parallel constitution that gives corporations more rights than real citizens? Wikileaks doesn't think so. Once again, Wikileaks is right on this point.

One potential problem Wikileaks must face is the perhaps mistaken perception that Assange operates with an anti-American bias. Since corruption and patronage networks are a world-wide problem, it behooves Wikileaks to be balanced in its exposure of unethical activities. In fact, the E.U. and especially China, not to mention Russia, which seems to operate in a rogue class all by itself, have their own huge problems with corruption fostered by insider patronage systems. It is true that Wikileaks also publishes information on European corruption. Nevertheless, in order to become fully credible, the Wikileaks leadership must also demonstrate that its revelations are far more than a special weapon of resentment against American problems and hypocrisies. Imagine, for instance, that Wikileaks would be equally persistent about releasing insider information exposing the criminality in the Swiss and Luxembourgian banking systems. Or even the activities--past and present--of a corporation such as Siemens...

The extent of the insiders' panic at the prospect that their secret activities could be open to public scrutiny can be gauged by the viciousness of the vendetta being directed against Wikileaks by the special-interest operatives in influence positions. It cannot be coincidental that a dropped rape charge against Julian Assange was rekindled in the immediate wake of the Wikileaks' release of confidential State Department documents. Immediately thereafter, in an obviously coordinated pressure campaign, Google, PayPal and MasterCard were somehow compelled to cease facilitating anything to do with Wikileaks. The point was to attack Wikileaks' funding stream. How effective is Wikileaks promising to be? Judging by this campaign to discredit the organization and its leader, Wikileaks threatens to be very effective indeed. Is that a bad thing?

The Wikileaks revelations should threaten neither a responsibly acting government nor a responsible corporation. In fact, the publication of State Department documents reveals a U.S. State Department that is for the most part professional and responsible. That is not a bad thing either. So what is the big fuss all about? It is primarily the power brokers within patronage systems that object to the publication of embarrassing material that should be public anyway. They may be most afraid of what Wikileaks has yet to publish—such as lists of key politicians with foreign bank accounts. These corporations and corporate executives that cheat by hiding taxable income in offshore activities, or by using accounting tricks, are also threatened by any development that might bring more transparency to their off-the-books operations. Count on it!

And what is the sordid response to Wikileaks revelations? By all means criminalize the people who stand for ethical scruples! Punish those people who don't play along with the sordid status quo. It is just another chapter in an old story acted out for the umpteenth time in history by unscrupulous insiders who want to protect their privileges.

L. D. Davidson is a Latin teacher and editor of *Antium*, a journal "rooted in reason and representing a vision of creative and intellectual substance amid the incoherence of the Present." He is also a regular contributor to the Op-Ed page of *The Sunday Gazette*.

~~~~~~~~~~~

Notable Mohawk Valley Quote

"I understand you have selected this locality [Amsterdam] because of its well known freedom from anarchy and rebellion, its air of provincial simplicity, its absence of prudishness and prussic acid temperaments, its psalmlike atmosphere, its charity, humility and penitence. All these we with proper humility and great reluctance and pride admit we possess. We are also singularly free from penuriousness.

The city's slogan is "Success is yours in Amsterdam," and success will be the lot of every man here if he plugs away, behaves himself and uses his brains...In its institutions for the public benefit, it invites comparison with the other cities. All in all, Amsterdam is a pretty good town. It has the right sort of people in it, people one can tie to, who are good friends and good neighbors, kind-hearted, sympathetic and helpful."

From an address to the 13th Rockefeller Family Association Meeting by Dr H. M. Hicks. *The Transactions of the Rockefeller Family Association, Volume 2.* Henry Oscar Rockefeller, et al.

~~~~~~~~~~~

one man, typing

jay towne

11/27/10

i guess it started with a dream. a dirty dream with my ex and me having sex in a tree, or so it seemed. and the thought of that encounter filled me with a sense of calm i've been hard pressed to attain these last few months. you see i'm losing my mind, i have
been for some years in a slow, certain progression marked by mental aberrations of all kinds: angry fits, delusional functioning, apparitions appearing, all melting into a lethargic semi-coma. (not all at once, you understand) so these last six months have been the cherry on the sundae of a mostly sad and ineffectual life.
and so i have this--an outlet for my growing insanity and a word processor that capitalizes my words if i don't.

i was watching tv and a commercial came on with mike and a girl and… i should say young woman, and the young woman said she wants to trade up, she wants to get to the next level, and i thought, yeah i'd like to get to the next level, i'd like to get to the next level, but, the next level kind of scares me. it keeps me from moving on to the next level, and just then the new hess truck commercial came on and i forgot everything else.

i went in to pee and a voice entered my head and asked me if i was going to pray while doing it. and i said of course, don't you think god planned for people to pray while peeing, since he created us with that potential? and isn't it written to pray without ceasing, and again to be constant in prayer and so i prayed "god, i thank you for everything you have given me, including my mind and, such as it is, my body. help me to use them for good not for ill and help me to be always thankful. in christ's name, amen."
long prayer – i really had to go. the other voice went away.

i want to say a few words about the way i treat people. first, if they are pretty, i treat them well; i dote on them; i worship them. if they are large i disdain them, i judge them, i condemn them. (i don't know where that comes from, maybe the evil one putting instantaneous thoughts in my head. i don't know.) if they are ugly, i recoil from them, and you know, i'm not pretty by any stretch. yet somehow i have this ugly, judgmental streak which attempts to kill any rapport with those people. i'm at a loss. i know and believe that everyone is created equal in god's eyes and that i should treat his children with a lot more respect then i do. i will continue to work on it because i want to be a person who is approved of god, no matter my tendencies.

the snow blew horizontal, whipped up by the fierce west wind, and stuck on fences and bushes and the side of my collar, framing my head in a damp, cold ring and dripping down melted onto my neck. there is something primal and joyous that moves me when i see the year's first snow. a sense of maybe being let out of school early to go play outside in it on the way home or maybe the sight of virgin flakes on a suicide mission.
i'm not sure. i know i'm not the only one, so stop giving me the stink eye.

all that effort, ruined by one ill placed sentence. pity

11/27/10

i am very active, it seems. walk to the thrift store to see mary lou and vinnie, (5 mins). walk to the post office (15 mins) walk to my housemate's house sitting job because we are on a break and she won't answer the phone because she is mad at me and i get visions of someone harming her and so i get worried when i don't hear from her and i know i shouldn't be so paranoid but i am (45 mins). it's important to stay active.

i have a lot of dreams…but i won't tell you any of them. you are going to have to guess.
nope, that's not it.

my faith is very important to me. i spent a portion of my day this sabbath reading the bible and bible based books and, if the truth be told, i needed twice or more what i spent.

which is to say i am devoted but not devoted enough to take the next step. i am fearful, i am halfhearted, i am weak and unstable. god sure does pick em!

i'm writing with my teeth in, trying them out for the first time with glue.
no i'm not...i am typing at the library because my computer has a malevolent virus in it (not a benevolent virus) so my planned outing with my teeth coincided with this attack from inside and my teeth stuck with me, not the computer. now the library has become my new, long lost old friend and their shiny new computers are my toys, and yes
they capitalize where not asked to do so.

the purpose of life is training. you are being trained for better things the moment you are cognizant, sometimes before. god's spirit moved upon the waters and dry land appeared, like our ego appears out of the primordial womb, ready to learn and tackle more and greater tasks until we are king of the hill in our lives. we are being shepherded through life, guided into making better and better decisions so that one day we will be able to accept the role of celestial being, accepting the responsibilities that living eternally puts forth.

i am going through a crisis of faith, of being. i tried a new medicine that ripped me up now i am withdrawing and i am surrounded by confusion, temptation and i am in shock the likes of which i have not known since the inception of my disease. god told me: when you go through deep rivers i will be with you... now i have to accept and believe.
the hardest thing i've ever done.

1/3/11

this thing is to record some of my conflicts with god, but since god has chosen to disown me, because of some sin, some magical sin i've been committing this past hour, then that is the way it goes.
it's easter weekend and i've been disowned by god because he doesn't like the fact that i have a different opinion than his, and he doesn't like me being a free moral agent, and he doesn't like me fornicating, which

doesn't really matter now because i don't fornicate anymore, except with myself, so this is what i am going to do i am going to lie to god in the morning, confess allmy terrible sins and ask forgiveness through christ, then i am going to go take communion IN VAIN, he could strike me down, he could disown me even further or he could even own up to his own promises and actually give me what i need but that would take too much effort for god, god doesn't like effort, he likes to sit back and get accolades from all his servile servants instead of free will accolades from free wills. so this thing i am holding is to record my thoughts especially when they are coming from god, so rapid fire that i can't write them down.

i hope god loves me but if he doesn't he can stick it up his ass i could give a fuck less.

so you're not going to give me a help mate. you're not going to give me a sex mate. i'll tell you what you are going to do, listen. this is god's plan for me: be celibate. oh like all those priests who are celibate, or just like some of the priests are celibate. you have a hand. you have a cock. you have lotion, use it.

so this is what you left for me, pain, anguish and more pain. since you couldn't do for me what you claim you can do, i am not giving to you what i could, which is devotion. so you know what your will is going to be to me now, after this? and you know what you will mean to me, now? zero. i will not change anything i do nor feel any guilt for anything. i'm going to stick to my particular sins and will feel not a tinge of guilt. i will give to you my discussions- no. my diatribes- no. i will give you what you gave me, rituals. because that is what you gave me, my guilt reducing rituals. a false religion. that is what you have given me, all, my life.

first what you do is inspire people everywhere to pray for you, asking for their particular needs to be met, then you disregard those prayers and do whatever the hell you want, because you are god and you can. so what is the purpose of this? nothing.

i have no one god. i have no one in this town. i have no one who loves me for who i am. you have successfully taken away the dream of having somebody, for the sake of me being...celibate. that is what paul said in your stinking bible. that is what you said in your stinking bible. that i need to be celibate. a catholic priest diddling girls and boys. amen to that.

when you can't coerce, you condemn. when you can't condemn, you kill. you don't help, you don't heal, you don't assist in any way.
it's not enough you took away my childhood. now you took away my sanity. you took away any chance at making a living. you took away my health. you took away my soul mates.
all of them. now you want to take away my life, because that is just the kind of god you are.
it is written, god is love. it is written, god is love.

you have put the hugest burden on me, as if my intelligence alone is going to be able to handle it. and the reason i broke down is that you broke down. and now i sit. watching television. eating ramen noodles. with no friends, no mate, just a couple of pets. even a felon gets visitors.

yeah you lost me. because you treat people like objects to do your bidding. and what have you done for me in forty years? nothing. i am still as bad off as i was when i started. you have given me nothing. the intelligence i have has always been there. so, you took me, an innocent child and you gave me rape, fondling, adultery, (oops that came later), victimization, objectification and you gave this to me for what purpose? ostensibly to teach me a lesson, to make me learn from life. great! you couldn't teach me like a normal parent would. give me good things, teach me good principles. so now what do we have? rape, abominations of every kind. and you want me to pray to you? to be thankful for my existence!? while i have no one and nothing? no future, a scarred past. this is your ideal life for me? it's no wonder i won't serve you.

it's pretty much like when i buy a lottery ticket, it's a chance that something might happen.
it's hope, belief and a wing and a prayer away from success. it's the same as when i visualize her- i pray to god, which is my ticket, i believe, sometimes, infrequently, which is my reward, which leaves

me with no real reward because i've already received what i wanted in my head.
not content to sit back and receive, i seek success through my own efforts, again, without god.

it's pitiful. if i had dedicated myself to my guitar i would, of course, been a master by now and had been receiving accolades galore. but, i guess, you can't fight destiny, especially if you are too thick to see it working in your life to begin with.

the sight of a woman is not enough
the feel of a woman is much too much
the dream of a woman is all i see
the scent of a woman is all i need

here's the transition:
i thought what i thought and what i thought was, temporarily, wrong
this vitriolic bastard, this pained soul that i was was angry and confused, like all children are at times, and like all children being carted around a store wanting daddy to buy them a treasured toy i wanted something, demanded something that wasn't due to be mine and threw a big, nasty, name calling, i'm deserting you you rapacious dick, fit. i am a crybaby and i admit it, now.
now i accept my limitations and god's lack of limitations and all that means for my life. period.

the look the glance
the life the dance
the look on her face
is the only trouble i need to get into
if we care enough to look our best
the lord will take care of all the rest

we surround ourselves
with all our petty problems
and this drama feeds on itself and
becomes the story of our lives
well, what happens if the story changes,
from somewhere outside of ourselves?

what happens if, in the end, we aren't who
we thought we were?
what happens if this happens now?

now is the time to part ways with myself, my former self
which dogs me at every turn
this time to eschew those former people, bad for me in every way,
my former friends
and everything bad for me, or wrong for me or former,
will be winnowed away, and now is the time to declare
my unrighteousness will cease,
my love of evil will cease
so here it is, my wake up call
for all to see
what is my intent in this world

pretty blonde woman, young, no umbrella, exits mall and stands there,
reaching for a phone
thin man, young at heart, exits mall, pauses, goes to woman, says-do
you need an umbrella?
she says dispassionately-mind your own fucking business
he pulls his backpack on, opens his black umbrella, says-whatever you
say lady, whatever you say, walks and skips and clicks his heels away
into the storm

if i avert my eyes i miss a glance
if i avert my eyes i miss a chance

ladies and gentlemen, honored guests, the invited and the disinvited
who came anyway.
you might notice i am wearing jeans on this, the happiest day of my
life. it's not a fashion statement, it's simply a testament of the vagaries
of life. you see, i, threw on my tuxedo trousers in a hurry, me being
late, and i ripped the zipper. no i didn't damage any of the goods,
my bride will be happy to hear. but i did manage to have a pair of
these jeans behind my seat in my truck, dirty from hunting, but
serviceable. so never fear where there is a will, there is a way,

so i'm told and here we are, me underdressed and she still willing...
what's that, hon... okay, whew!...don't scare me like that... she still
willing. let's get the show on the road!

in subtle days, in subtle ways
when hands twist the hands that heal
salvation comes in tens and ones
when you lose all of your appeal

this is how i wound up crazy, god. reading and re-reading this word,
constantly, without breaks or outlet. is that what you want? this
incessant voice driving me to study until i lose it?
heaven help me or my family if you drive me to the brink again

i'll tell you my role in this world: if you walk dogs, as i do, you'll
notice an unfortunate by-product of feeding them is that they poop and
you can never pick up all the poop, there is still a residue left after,
which, after one day the flies descend on it and after the second day
the flies have moved on and what you have left is me, the latest picked
over poop stain on this world's grass.

in passing...
the way a falcon in flight dips and dives to avoid the attack of a
smaller bird
the way a shirtless man in high heels and belly struggles to close the
blinds on an otherwise open second story window
the way the grass grows strong next to a struggling tombstone
the way a squirrel chatters in the boughs of an oak, threatening the
impending rain

mostly i think my life is good...i walk to work...to the bank, to the
store...my job is okay...money is okay, more than i expected...maybe
a vacation upcoming...pets okay...she's okay, so far...basically okay.

i have this pressure in my head, my heart and it would be just like me
to think that i am so important as to warrant a "sign" from god with
this and to think it portends more than just a headache or angina

(the bells of st. stan's ring out)

that's always nice, one of the reasons we love it here, look, i am not
trying to make great art here, just trying to express myself, people
don't understand they think i'm different, special, but i'm not, just a
little touched by god, that's all, could be anybody really, been this way
all my life, but i guess, we all have a role to play, a role of our own
choosing, our choices become what we should have chosen after all,
our destiny, my choice is yours, but enough of this crap, the point is,
listen to those bells, the best thing in this place…

in my dream i held a pretty blonde girl, thin with glasses
i put her down on the ground and i was hard on her
and i said do you feel that and she said yes
and she said do you feel the footsteps of my boyfriend
coming up behind you
and i said yes
but will i do without the thought of you

i don't know where god is but i know where he isn't- he isn't
redeeming me, filling my heart with joy or gladness, in fact i don't
think i have ever experienced joy in my life and i would if he were
busy finding her for me, wouldn't i? and there is no sense complaining
it only makes it worse. if you ask anything in my name i will rape you,
abuse you and confound you, that's the news i get. so now what?

…because i learned early on that there were two sides to this life: the
right side and the wrong side and i knew by observation that the
people perpetrating this pain on me were working on the wrong side
and that, by intuition, since there was evil, there had to be good
somewhere and i needed to be on the right side to outlast this pain.
now since, i have dabbled in this evil and recently shed it completely
so now what? am i redeemed? am i saved? am i cured of this residual?
no. i am in the process and that is all i can speak to and god save me i
am hopeful…

i see them walking through the cemetery hand in hand and i wish it
were me but i know he is better suited to her and why would i want her
anyway when i am waiting for the one better suited to me and i can't,
after all, have more than my allotted one can i, i mean, c'mon.

i have been run over so many times, been fired again and again, flown
repeatedly across the country in so many permutations of the same
inspiration and what is it doing for me save annoying me? i can't say.
i'm shifting gears, letting these thoughts subside and the message
abide in me, like a parent with an unruly child.

i think to my ex-girlfriends i was like the toy dog that pisses on shoes
and who everyone pets and calls "big boy" just to boost his little ego.

asshole stepping up to a stall at the farmers market:
-do you have anything with high fructose corn syrup in it, 'cuz that's
what i'm used to
-how much is that cucumber? i'm teaching a sex ed class
-what does organic mean, anyway?

i would have been all right talking to the guy at the stationery store but
as i was walking up my schlong popped through the slit in my boxers
and just stood there so i felt compromised and couldn't adjust

no, god, if we are going to have a breakthrough i am going to
document it…
i can't fathom why i am the way i am, i mean, i know i did my share of
corrupting myself but where the hell were you why didn't you take
control? i asked you time and again, don't tell me i didn't mean it so
you didn't. i know, free moral agents and all that. like i said, i didn't
help matters being me. water under the bridge, i guess.

not a bad day for not finding your house- i mean soul mate. did i say
housemate? i guess i'd better hurry home!

i am the king of the ugly women. they crowd around me like a homely
harem, viciously patrolling, threatening to cut any pretty woman who
tries to take away their jay, king of their nights, lord of their days

…after the earthquake came a fire, but the lord was not in the fire, then
after the fire came a gentle whisper…

am i to understand that i am to remain functionally celibate until the
resolution of this dream?

well that's grand isn't it, for you maybe. you get enforced chastity and
all it's pious aftereffects
i get frustration and virtual castration and i'm not a priest? what
benefits do i reap except sleepless nights visualizing and an increased
empathy? c'mon tell me...

people here think i'm one-dimensional. well, i'm not. i have loved. i
have lost. i have feelings and other emotions. i have theories and
theorems. i teach, i preach, i love, i despise.
i lust. i have and don't have sex. they think because i crack some jokes
that that is all i am?

now why would she back up the opposite way and drive down there
when she knows it's blocked off and she would have to come back this
way anyway, just to avoid seeing me and little misha? that's asinine.
does she know it's blocked off? maybe. i guess i'll give her the benefit
of the doubt. look, here she comes, wave!

the day ends and night falls
and i draw the curtains
she leaves, i remain
resolving nothing
(whispering) i have a girlfriend. she lives in my wallet. i cut her out of
a magazine. she has a big straw hat and a big wide white smile. closed
eyes but i'm sure they're blue. she has dirty blonde hair, not dyed.
small, perfect breasts bulging in a tight fitting knit bikini top and she is
on a beach, looking up at the sun. next to rebecca she is the most
beautiful, perfect girl i have ever seen so now i have two imaginary
women in my life: one that inhabits my daydreams continuously and
one that lives in my wallet. pathetic.

purify me and i will be clean
wash me and i will be whiter than snow
oh give me back my joy
you have broken me
now let me rejoice
psalms 51:7-8

when i betray god, i betray myself

when i sin, i hurt myself
when i do what i do just to do it, i do what is wrong
and wound my own soul
when i act only for self, my actions defend the right
for god is not mocked and cannot be tempted

the pain i feel is the pain i inflict
the pain i inflict is the pain i accept
the pain i accept is the pain i redeem

god, i don't need this anymore this drama drama drama everywhere
and not a thought to think
i wallow in it night and day in one ear and out the other melodrama
pervades my head and i milk it for all it's worth not worth a damn it
comes out in my stupid poems and in all my writing
must be a better way - transcend i suppose or just ignore like people
ignore me 'cuz they are sick of me spouting off about oh my troubles
are so bad or oh my troubles will be the death of me bunch of shit
never thought i'd be this way my life filled with so much f-ing me

the idiot box is an endless churning cesspool of filth, melodrama, lies
and untruth and they're not always the same and attachment to sin and
evil and it is a waste of time to watch it, it gives you nothing, and is
not beneficial except the shows on economics and sesame street

having said that, lets watch some tv!

in the search for pussy, a man will go to any lengths to uncover
himself
in the search for success, a man will go to any lengths to push himself
in the search for romance, a man will go to any lengths to reveal
himself
in the search for hegemony, a man will go to any lengths to free
himself
in the search for clarity, a man will go to any lengths to avoid himself
in the search for creativity, a man will go to any lengths to feed
himself
and in the search for immortality, nothing a man does really matters

in this search for my mate i am at a distinct disadvantage:
i don't have a pretty face
i have no teeth
i am out of shape
my mind malfunctions
i have no car
i have very little money
so what little that is out there for me
is not out there for me, it's out there for a better me, or that is
it's out there for somebody else

if it were up to me i would have a semi-nice job making semi-nice
money
live in a semi-nice house
have semi-nice friends
and go on semi-nice vacations with
the woman of my dreams, perfect love
perfect breasts
perfect life

am i depressed, sanguine, recalcitrant, apprehensive, mis-
apprehensive, adulterated, abominated, bromated, monochromated,
fish netted- sorry, that was just a mistake-i am melancholy for the first
time in years, because of my meds or that i fear for my future or i am
whimsical in my old age thinking- heavens!- what will people or the
pope do without me and how will they go on!! bullshit. i am just being
creative and i am wondering how i got here

so i asked god for help because i know he is apt to help me and he has
set everything up to benefit me and i begged and cajoled and pleaded
for help and i just checked the ticket and
IT IS A FOUR DOLLAR WINNER! now in my pathetic mind i'm
thinking, wow, this worked so why don't i ask for something better
like a lexus or a soul-mate or something and then i'm thinking better
not push him, he might bite be

i am alone with myself all day everyday and that
is fine except for all these thoughts i think
and these dreams i dream

and these loathsome feelings
and this disease
when i get home from work today
i am going to put my feet up
and i am not going to think, or talk or be -
hold on that's not right
i am going to think, talk and be
but i am going to put my feet up

what if i don't want to write it?
what if you give me a word of knowledge and i flat out
don't want to write it? thunderbolt? earthquake?
okay, the spirit of the prophets are subject to the prophets
and it's not like i don't want to, it's just a for instance
heaven help me if i don't want to write it, huh?

suppose you had a vision of meeting your soul-mate at work
and now you are at work and your soul-mate is at the counter, making
plans
with somebody else
would you rush in, declare them wrong,
declare your vision
and what story would you have?

this night belongs to us
to the way we are
to the tokens of sanity
we collect
tell it walking

i have boundaries, i have cataclysms, i have neuroses, i have
ideologies, i have perversities,
and now i have to tie my shoe

i have a healthy respect for the beautiful and an unholy attachment to
the lustful
i have an ecstatic affection for the wonderful and a dark reliance on
the dutiful

god i need you there for me,
if you aren't there i will be sunk
i need you more than i need food in my gut
more than shoes on my feet
more than my hands on my dick
i need you to supplant that evil vision
of self and sin with one of purity and peace
i need you god
don't make me repeat myself

let us proclaim this mystery of faith:
god eternal,
who created all
came down and created a vessel to live in personally,
lived purely, justly, then died
carrying the world's burdens back to himself
and will return soon (?)
bearing salvation, peace and vengeance
to our very aware planet
unwanted by most
caring for the right for all
in an absence of thought a new thought grows
how it is wrought nobody knows
what it has bought no one can tell
what is has caught- o bloody hell!
this bulllshit again jay? c'mon!
what can we know of what we know?
we cannot tell origins
we cannot sense truth except divinely
we cannot see duty from the routine

god, what if that image you gave me of my soul-mate is just a
construct of my sub-conscious, a picture of my purest likes or desires
for a mate? what if she isn't red haired but blonde, black or brunette?
and what if she isn't thin and pretty but large with no teeth? what then,
god? i might well be looking in the wrong place, for the wrong girl
and in vain. do you really think i need another "in vain" attached to
anything i do?

setup: library employee at break time in break room

-look out the window, jay
-yes god
-all this will be yours one day
-great- a parking lot, a few cars and two overweight women. is this my kingdom?
-i'm working on it

it's not just that this is the best, most creative time of my life. it's also filled with hope and some despair, a smattering of sin and conquests galore and now i am poised for greater success.
and it would be all fine and good but for this lack, this intuitive connection. i don't see god clearly, that is my fault, and i can't see my way to devote myself to the needful, instead rather i fill my head with the false and the spurious instead of being mindful.
any suggestions?

so when we tell our children they were conceived in room ten twenty six of the contemporary
resort hotel, the magic kingdom, they can then return twenty years later, like salmon to spawn,
to the same hotel, the same room and conceive for themselves. carry on the tradition.

i'm recording this because i want to. right now i am talking to god. god and i talk all day, every day, like you and i talk. he tells me things, i tell him things. sometimes i yell at him. he doesn't yell back but we hash it out. right now i have something to say: god, you know and i know that you are never going to give a woman to spawn with; this is just a ruse before you chop my head off. i'm serious! this is the way i think, sue me. i know you understand me, i get it but will i get it? the promised dame, the legs spread, the eyes, the hair. sorry. just asking. thanks for your restraint.

i move on, from her, black hair
laughing in the wind
i move on from her blonde hair
getting into the spoonful

of ice cream while she kisses me with her mouth
i move on, her brunette hair languishing on my face
while she inspects my eyes
i push on past this,
forfeiting past for present
excellence for immediacy

it is impossible for a limited mind to grasp the unlimited
unless the limited mind is blessed
god is right there! i see him. (i don't see him, i sense him)
i know what he wants, he wants to heal us and help us
to understand and care
he's taught me that through hardship and pain
gifts of success and heartfelt joy
this is the thing-
to see and know requires love of truth, sincerity and dedication
and an open mind can flourish with those

damn! i missed her. what time is it? eight forty-one. so tomorrow i will
be here at eight thirty-seven. look at her! she's getting into her car and
driving away! doesn't she know who i am? doesn't she know who she
could've met and what i could do for her?

i'm walking past the park hill adult home and i am talking into this
recorder so that when i pass the office window the people in there will
see me and think i am doing important work talking into my recorder
and they will think i am important going past them every day dressed
nicely and they will regret not hiring me when they could have and i
will have my revenge making nine dollars an hour twenty hours a
week at a job i love and they will think i am important

every now and then i don't want to listen to my recorder i just want to
create so i sit and scribble or type and i say out loud i love life! or how
are you doing i wish you well! so you see it sucks to be me with all
this sameness and irritability running through my head and all this me

why walk in the cemetery when you could walk the streets of
amsterdam. you can see row upon row of multi-colored mausoleums
with their ship lap artificial siding and their guests entombed, living

their lives unaware of the impending. why walk through the cemetery when you can meet the living dead on the streets of amsterdam.

lonely summer walking
dressing for cars and the women in them
hoping against hope that one of them
would turn and say let's give it a go!
not really what i want but
it's the sentiment i'm after

i met my love on pulaski street.
i went walking past the ukrainian catholic church.
and on the corner of pulaski and edwards there she was,
selling ice cream and sundries on a sunny day.
she wore a see through yellow topped white skirt and purple
converse high tops.
she saw me and began pushing her cart clackity-clack up the
broken and disheveled sidewalk.
i followed, bearing down
catching her quickly
do you have any shaved ice, i asked
melted, she said, go away
any soda, i asked
fizz is gone, she said, go away
will you marry me, i asked
she stopped and turned, put her hand
on my face, sighed, why didn't you say that
in the first place
then turned, faded away into the sun
clackitiy-clack

this is how it's worked thus far: you bless me, i reject or ignore you, i sin and you retreat, i sin more you disavow me until finally i need you and you are not near, which would be fine, the results of my sin and all that, but, when do you act gracious to me? when i'm destroyed and that starts the whole process again. why not grab me and hold me for dear life and give me the strength to do the same for you? isn't that the way it's supposed to be?

in my dream i was in a hotel room and the
pretty brunette clerk was in my room asleep
on the pullout cot and on her and littered
through out the room were countless
stuffed animals, mostly bunnies
and the clerk woke up, put her hand on my shoulder and asked
my name, and i said i'm nobody
go back to sleep

wish and hope
and dream and pray
and wish and hope
and dream and pray
and try to stand another day
without a poem or word to say
and not a sin that you betray

the thuds of pain hitting the floor
she screeching
he defending and threatening
child hiding from another
they shift and move
pounding footfalls mark the intensity
another two a.m. ritual

i like to drive people crazy cuz then they can join me

today is a great day, a stupendous day, because this day is the first in
almost two months that i have left the house and known for certain
that i locked the front door.

my lack of faith muzzles me. i am hamstrung by this certain inability
to trust and so everything and everyone suffers. i am getting better, but
getting better only works in the longest of long term scenarios and i
am in short term theory liability mode right now. i know god will help
me, but i must believe and i am getting older by the day.

sleeping upright, i can't stop coughing and my roommate can't sleep
so i am banished to the couch, this recorder in my hands my only link
to sanity, in the dark, fumbling for buttons i opine between breaths

there is nothing like the tales of the dead, i think, walking through the
cemetery on my way home, the walking dead that litter the streets of
this city, knowing or accepting nothing of their fate, to wind up here,
encased in mud and eternity, caring nothing for the pain and triumph
they must endure, passing through like the wind and with that this has
become overblown and senseless and not at all what i intended...

there's the man who bought chips and a dubious looking container of
salsa for his housemate and, against his better judgment, dipped his
chip in the salsa and ate it, thinking, if she gets sick, i get sick

i can satisfy my needs and whims but i cannot satisfy this desire to be
better than i am

i take for granted i can walk, to the store to the library to work.
i take advantage of that every day.
i take advantage of my ability to write and talk of my stupid-ass
feelings all day every day.
i take for granted that i can think or pray or feel. i take advantage of
that all day every day.
i take for granted that i am

she comes around the corner walking briskly, flush, cane in her hand
moving constantly, dull red rucksack on her back, the windows of the
store front look down on her, mockingly, she approaches and slows,
looks up at me behind dark sunglasses and says, jay, this outward
appearance merely hides me, it matters little to me and i say, nor to
me, as i bend to kiss her on the cheek, then pass her by

dead, dead
the bells ring
from his bed
the angels sing

this is a trustworthy saying and everybody should accept it: christ
jesus came into the world to save sinners, and i am the worst of all. but
god had mercy on me so that christ jesus could use me as a prime
example of his great patience with even the worst sinners, then others
could realize that they too could believe in him and receive eternal
life. that is my message, that is my life's work and if you don't accept
this, i'm sorry. for you.

-jerry where are you?
-i'm on the beach at sacandaga lake watching the boats run through the
water
-good. jonathan, how about you?
-i'm on a beach on cape cod, watching all the co-eds prance and
mingle
-okay. marcus, where are you?
-i'm on a beach at the south of france, watching all the topless woman
run up and down, and
 then this pretty tanned bitch comes over, stands over me and says, you
want some you
american stud, then rips off her bottoms and…
-marcus! that's quite enough…

i guess i need to stop being mean to my housemate or i am going to
find myself in my broken down studio apartment, nothing but nutmeg
to eat, no furniture, sitting on a milk crate in the middle of my "living
room" just me with my hair as my only guest

the other day…
hold on, i'm not done:
i am a stalker
i am a stalker
i'm not a stalker
i'm not a stalker
every man's a stalker
every man's a stalker
i'm not a murderer
i'm not a murderer
the other day i dreamt, i mean daydreamed i was driving a stock car in
the daytona five-hundred and i was driving and i led the pack for

awhile and then i pitted and wound up behind, which pissed me off, so
this driver cut me off and i took him out… but did you see me on
speed channel, or espn? am i a stock car driver because i had ideations
but didn't actually drive? do i have to say it?

when doing laundry it's always underwear that falls to the floor
when doing homework- who am i kidding? i haven't done homework
since nineteen eighty-three
or for that matter, laundry

the case for canned fruit

i am hungry and
i am waiting for my ramen noodles to "cook"
looking in the cupboard and i see
oatmeal, dehydrated milk and a half-used peanut butter jar
on my shelf, alone

it's really up to you, i guess
you are the potter, we are the clay
the work of your hands
and if you see fit
if it's in your will
that a young girl gets kidnapped,
taken into the woods, raped and killed or
that a young boy gets tied up
and butchered in the suburbs
i guess that's your will too, huh?

rebuttal

i am a god who loves-
it is my essence to love all creatures
i have created or caused to be created.
if you think i cause, arrange or take any
pleasure in the pain or death of one of my little
ones, you are terribly mistaken and you impugn me
greatly.
love bears all things, believes all things, hopes all things,

endures all things. love never fails. i never fail. it's only you
who fail. to love. to seek. to see. to believe and to trust me.

it doesn't really matter-
if i don't choose it, you don't get it
and it doesn't really matter-
if you don't choose it, i don't get it
supreme being versus human will
which is stronger?

i may have just screwed up my destiny. i think she just went in to the
library and i chose to go home instead. she may have been in the post
office and i just walked on by. she nay have been in one of those cars
that just passed and i waved to the wrong one. so here i am walking
home and maybe she lives on this street...

what's it going to take, god, for you to get off your ass and get into my
heart?

i said, i am one-hundred percent honest and open to you and to
everyone
she said, bullshit, nobody can be
i said, try me
and she said, does this dress make my butt look fat?

seven years! seven years we've been broken up and this is where i am?
i love her, not that way, she loves me, not that way, and we go along
living together like we are semi-family. this is crazy. i need a date. i
need a place of my own. i need to shut up or she will hear me.

thus begins the temptation...will i fold, will i scold, will i die if truth
be told? will i yield, will i feel, will i wish that she were real?

god, what i'm saying is if you are going to make me do that then it's a
shortcut to making me what i used to be, with my transitional-
situational ethics and selling out and i will not let it happen again. but
if you tell me it will happen with her just the way you showed me then
i can sign on to that, do you know what i mean?

-that was cool! (pause) you are so wise. like some smart guy only with
a big dick.
-a dick you love, right?
-you got it.
-look, you and i both know we have a short shelf life. pretty soon you
are going to get bored with me and go seeking out other men and
that's fine, if you want to use me as a stepping stone that's fine, i
won't begrudge you that at all, just give me fair warning so you don't
break my heart.
-i could never break your heart.
-yes you could and you will. but i don't mind.
-let me show you what i will.

no rhymes except the ones i had
no words of truth or light to add
my steps are firm my mind is strong
they guard me as i walk along
no loves or other debts to pay
i stand at the encroaching day
and say these words to open air
and wear these clothes, ignore the tear
whatever

what to say, what to say?
first i'd like to thank all my fans, the voting members of the academy,
and all my fans, and god who loved me and inspired me, my teachers,
my family that supported me and all that nonsense for help making me
what i am,
a big fat loser who made it big by figuring out which side his bread
was buttered and sticking with the right pony.
thank you, thank you very much.

i need to turn this freakin' tv off
i am lying on the couch, trying to sleep
i thought it would keep me company, but no
it's an annoying intrusion
i am in an existential crisis, i don't need
to hear about hamburgers and fries
i'm not avoiding her

i'm not walking fast for her
i'm not taking off my clothes for her or
taking off her clothes for her
if she loves me she does
and if not so be it
i'm just living day to day, hour to hour
like everyone else who has no hope

i'm rejected but not pathetic
(i'm pathetic but not because i'm rejected)
i'm pathetic but not victimized
i'm victimized but not regretful
i'm regretful but not remorseful
i'm remorseful but not despondent
and i am not helpless

god, you have primed me for great joy
but if you are going to prime me for great joy
and not give it to me then
kill me now, because i am not going
to tolerate that bullshit otherwise
my entire life has been one long preparation for greatness.
from writing plays in school
to dealing with criminals all my life to loving and leaving all those
women, i have been trained
to manipulate people and events in my life for my personal benefit.
now god is doing it for me and what better! the creator orchestrating
my success, at nobody's
expense. amazing! now all i have to do is unlearn all that i have
learned in order to facilitate my
untoward transformation from evil liar to righteous expediter, and
that without remedy.
hallelujah!

i dared the bumblebee to sting me and it did
i dared the ox to gore me and it did
i cursed a star and it spat on me
i'm living a lie and everyone knows
and nobody knows

and that is what i know
this evening, walking
you can hide behind the argument of your needs
you can hide behind the argument you must be free
you can hide behind the argument of this is the way it should be,
or could be

but the fact remains
if you choose god's will, you do god's will
if you refuse god's will, you do god's will
either way
what happens, is god's will
what doesn't happen is god's will
there is no fighting, there is no argument
sufficient to absolve you
unless you choose
i am walking to save my life
i am walking to get a better view
i am walking because i have nothing and time
is not my friend
i have no car, i have no life
i have no love
what does that mean to me?
it means that all arguments and rationalizations
are of no effect and that i must face this
what does that mean to you?
absolutely nothing

Jay Towne has been writing poems and stories since grade school but has only recently been published in *Capital Region Poets Magazine*. He has an unorthodox style and has never gotten a bad review of his work, but is braced for whatever might come. His first book of poetry, *a thorough avoidance*, is due to be published soon and will be available for sale at The Book Hound in Amsterdam. *One man, typing* is an excerpt of a planned full length book with the same name. He currently resides in Amsterdam, NY.

Notable Mohawk Valley Quote

Crane Street, Schenectady runs all the way to Burma

"If you could be someplace else right now,
Charlie, where would it be?

I don't know. A football game.
How about you?

If I had my choice
I'd be sitting on a nice, soft stool...
in the National Press Club in Washington, D. C...
surrounding a tall, cold bourbon and soda.

What? I didn't know newspapermen drank.

How about you?

A place you probably never heard of.
Cannonball Island in Central Park.

Really? New York?

Yeah, Schenectady, New York.
They have a central park, too,
with this island in the middle.
Sort of take your girl there
if you're real friendly.

Sounds all right.
I have a lot of friends in Schenectady.

- No kidding.

Yeah. My column is syndicated there,
The Gazette. Your folks live there?

My father has a grocery store
on Crane Street, by the locomotive works.

Really? Where'd you go to school?

- Union College.
I'm supposed to be a schoolteacher.
After the war I have an appointment.
History teacher in Pleasant Valley High School.

That's fine. Your folks will get
quite a kick out of reading about you.

You mean all that stuff
will be in the Schenectady paper?

Sure. You don't mind, do you?

Heck no.
What do you know.
It's a small world, isn't it?

Yes, and it's getting smaller.
If only more folks back home would realize…
Crane Street, Schenectady
runs all the way to Burma…
this would be the last war.

Amen."

From the Film *Objective Burma* (1945) written by Ranald MacDougall (March 10, 1915 - December 12, 1973). Born in Schenectady, New York, MacDougall began his career ushering at Radio City Music Hall. He then sought work elsewhere in Rockefeller Center as a staff writer for NBC Radio before becoming a film director who directed, among others, Joan Crawford in *Queen Bee* He also wrote the screenplays for *Mildred Pierce* (1945), *The Unsuspected* (1947), *June Bride* (1948), and *The Naked Jungle* (1954).

Recommended Reading

Around Caroga Lake, Canada Lake, And Pine Lake. Images of America. By Carol Parenzan Smalley. (Charleston, SC: Arcadia Publishing, 2011). 128 pp. $21.99. (paperback).

Along New York's Route 20. Postcard History Series. By Michael J. Till. (Charleston, SC: Arcadia Publishing, 2011). 128 pp. $21.99. (paperback).

Smoke under Vroman's Nose. A Photographic Memoir of Railroading and Everyday Life in the Schoharie Valley. By Len Kilian. (Rotterdam Junction, NY: ELESKAY, 2011). 80 pp. $35 (hard cover).

Amsterdam. Postcard History Series. By Gerald R. Snyder and Robert von Hasseln. (Charleston, SC:Arcadia Publishing, 2011). 128 pp. $21.99. (paperback).

Little Falls. Images of America. By Susan R. Perkins and Caryl A. Hopson. (Charleston, SC: Arcadia Publishing, 2010). 128 pp. $21.99. (paperback).

Off Kilter. A Woman's Journey To Peace With Scoliosis, Her Mother & Her Polish Heritage. By Linda Wisniewski. (Nashville, TN: Pearlsong Press, 2008. 158 pp. $18.95. (paperback).

The Erie Canal Through Saratoga County. By Amelia T. O'Shea (Freehold, NY: Amelia T. O'Shea, 2007). 150 pp. $18.00 (spiral bound paperback).

Toward Civic Integrity Re-establishing the Micropolis. By Vincent DeSantis. (Troy, NY: Troy Book Makers, 2007). 260 pp. 14.95 (paperback).

The Long Emergency: Surviving the End of Oil, Climate Change, and Other Converging Catastrophes of the Twenty-First Century. By James Howard Kunstler. (NY, NY: Grove Press, 2006). 336 pp. $14.95 (paperback).

Upstream is supported solely by The Book Hound. Please support The Book Hound in order to keep *Upstream* going.

The Book Hound
16 E. Main St.
1st Floor
Amsterdam, NY 12010
518 842-7504

Hours
Tues-Fri Noon-5
Sat 11-3

www.thebookhound.net

The Book Hound is a used and antiquarian bookstore with reasonably priced books in all categories. Our prices are generally less than the lowest priced booksellers on the internet.

While The Book Hound stocks books in all categories, our specialties are New York State books, American History, Children's books, religious books and non-fiction.

Additional copies of *Upstream,* as well as many of the books mentioned in it, can be ordered from The Book Hound or on our website www.thebookhound.net. Check out *Upstream's* blog at www.upstreamjournal.wordpress.com.

Made in the USA
Charleston, SC
15 August 2011